A FAMILY SURVIVAL KIT

(formerly
A Survival Kit for Wives)

*HOW TO
AVOID
FINANCIAL
CHAOS
BEFORE
TRAGEDY
STRIKES*

by
Don & Renee
Martin
with
Joan Scobey,
editor

VILLARD BOOKS   NEW YORK 1988

CONTENTS

*III*PROTECTING YOUR ASSETS

*IV*HOW TO SURVIVE PRACTICALLY ANYTHING

WORKBOOK

SPECIAL EDITION FOR FIRST NATIONWIDE NETWORK CUSTOMERS

This special version of *The Family Survival Kit* was produced by First Nationwide Network and is available only through financial institutions belonging to the Network.

The First Nationwide Network is the nation's largest organization of independent, locally owned and managed financial institutions. With more than 750 branches in more than 35 states, Network members pool professional resources to bring their customers valuable banking products, such as national check-cashing privileges and account-relocation services. This book is part of the Network's continuing commitment to assist customers by providing important consumer financial information.

The consumer financial education programs have been designed to meet numerous needs, yet all share a single goal: to help consumers understand their financial options so they may make the wisest personal choices. These efforts include funding of the National Public Television series *Take Charge!* by the First Nationwide Network, as well as financial management classes including "Buying a Home," "Borrowing Wisely" and "Managing Your Cash." Additionally, the book *Financing Matters* was produced and published by the First Nationwide Network and Ford Motor Credit Company.

INTRODUCTION

Can you answer these questions:

- What are your assets? How much are they worth?
- Do you know how to get a loan? Could you qualify for one?
- Who has access to your safe-deposit box? Where is the key?
- Will your children have money for college if your family income drops?
- How do you get emergency cash if your spouse is out of town or becomes ill?
- Will your medical insurance cover a long-term illness?
- How much life insurance does your spouse have? Where are the policies?
- Where is your spouse's will? What does it say?

If you answered "no" or "I don't know" to any of these you're in good company. Most of us are woefully disorganized about vital family information. We know where the safe-deposit box is, but we've lost track of the key—or who can use it. We pay life insurance premiums, but we don't know what the policies are currently worth—or if they still cover us adequately. We have medical insurance, but we don't know if it includes a long-term disability. We don't even know how much we're worth. Most of us know just enough to lull us into a false sense of security, and security—your family's security—is precisely what is at risk.

Most of us muddle along until something jolts us into action. In our case, it was a car accident. We weren't in it, thank goodness, but it shattered the lives of two of our good friends. John was killed outright, and Betty was so badly injured she was hospitalized for almost a year. We're not sure when—or if—she'll recover completely.

Their tragic accident shocked us—and it unnerved us. What if that had happened to us? Who would take care of our children? Would our friends even know whom to notify? We took long hard looks at our family arrangements. We thought we were pretty savvy about them, but there were still loose ends we hadn't considered. The most important was that our children wouldn't have adequate information about our family's household business. From that terrible accident we were learning some valuable lessons, the hard way.

As we tried to help Betty, we found ourselves making lists, getting information for her lawyer, her doctors, her insurance broker. We began to see just what you'd need to get your family's business in order, in this or any other emergency. Our lists turned into worksheets, and the information into guidelines; we put them all away for our own future reference. By this time we were working at least as hard for our own protection as for Betty's.

One evening at dinner we met a woman who had been widowed a few years ago. We told her about our project.

"Oh, how I wish I'd had a workbook like that before my husband died," she said. "What trouble it would have saved me with probate, Rob's business partners, just everything. Our affairs were a mess!"

And that's how we started *A Family Survival Kit*.

Most people aren't prepared for the event they fear most: the death or illness of their spouses. Even a psychologist we interviewed, who readily understands the process of denial in her patients, ironically couldn't help herself. "When Arnie first got sick, we didn't want to talk about it," she told us. "We were afraid that if we put his affairs in order, then it would really happen."

Women, especially, were terrifyingly ignorant about their economic status. "For five years after my husband died, I had no idea of my financial situation," a California widow told us. "I was living in limbo until the estate was settled."

People who do have resources often lack the skills and financial knowledge to ensure their long-term economic survival. "My wife left me $300,000 in insurance, and I didn't have the faintest idea what to do with it," said a schoolteacher. "What's worse, I was besieged with conflicting advice."

Among the people we interviewed, the most common and painful reaction was the paralyzing inability to make important decisions when they were first engulfed by the trauma of widowhood or divorce, or burdened by a seriously ill or disabled spouse. "For months after Mark died, I didn't know whether to sell the house or not," says a Texas journalist. "I couldn't even decide whether to sell his car or mine."

As we talked to more and more newly single people, we began to get an important message. As unsettling as it may have been to talk about death and divorce, they claimed it was more terrifying not to be prepared for them. "Don't wait till it happens!" they told us urgently, time after time.

We also discovered that when you get your family's business in order, and know how to handle difficult situations when they arise, some splendid things can happen. Universally, everyone feels a wonderful sense of self-sufficiency, independence, strength, and competence.

The promise of *A Family Survival Kit* is peace of mind. It offers an emotional life raft of knowledge and preparation that will see you through any crisis, and the reassurance that comes from safe-guarding your family's legacy and preventing a future financial disaster.

A Family Survival Kit will help you organize all your family's essential information sensibly and efficiently. Its unique format is your tailor-made kit for economic survival. The text is a reference library of expert advice on the financial, legal, and practical realities of taking care of the business of your family. The Workbook section at the end of the book becomes a permanent archive of your essential family information—just as soon as you fill it in. This detachable section has clear, simple worksheets on which to record all the indispensable information about your family's most important papers and private business, checklists to remind you of what to do in an emergency, and information sheets to help you do it.

Using the Worksheets

Most of us respect books too much to write in them. That's why *A Family Survival Kit* is in the form of a workbook. We invite you to write in it. We beg you to write in it. The best way to honor the intent of *A Family Survival Kit* is to make notes on its pages, underline its text, make computations in the margins. And especially, fill in the worksheets and checklists. Use it.

This book is designed to be easy to use. You'll find all the worksheets in the last section of the book. Each one is titled, numbered, and cross-referenced to its explanatory text so you can flip back and forth between the body of the book and the worksheets.

The entire Workbook section is perforated so you can store it in your safe-deposit box, duplicate it for other members of your family or your advisors, or just take certain worksheets with you when you meet with your advisors. It also allows you to complete the forms while they're still in the book, or detach them first if that's easier for you.

As you read the text, you'll note that some information should be updated periodically. This means you'll need additional copies of those worksheets for the future. Before you use any worksheet, duplicate it so you'll always have at least one blank copy in reserve—do it right from the book, or detach the page first.

Getting Started

The hardest thing about getting started is . . . getting started. If preparing for a tragedy before it happens puts you off, consider instead the happier benefits of having your family records in order. That's what occurred to our friend Dorothy, who wants to open a retail shop. "As soon as I fill out the worksheets on my assets and net worth," she said gleefully, "I bet the bank will talk to me more seriously about a loan."

Most people won't have the data to complete a net worth statement—or a lot of other family records, either—on their own. Husbands and wives need to pool their knowledge. Each wage earner and each bill payer has essential information to contribute. Sometimes the larger family wage earner—and let's face it, that's usually the man—will resist sharing financial and legal records. And that's understandable. This is a topic that can be uncomfortable.

We know many husbands who've said, "Well, you know my accountant knows everything, my attorney knows everything, just talk to them if anything happens."

One wife replied, "I realize that your attorney and your accountant know everything, but I feel so insecure. I'd really feel a lot better if I understood enough to know what questions to ask them."

Another told her reluctant husband, "I wouldn't want my ignorance to destroy what you've built up. One way of avoiding that is to learn a little more about what's going on, so I can protect your interests."

A third wife, who felt strongly about being responsible for herself as a woman, simply said to her husband, "I'd like to learn more about the financial affairs of our household. I just realized I want to take more responsibility in our partnership." He was surprised by the depth of her commitment, she reported, and pleased. "I felt a little like Eliza Dolittle triumphantly becoming a 'consort battleship' to Henry Higgins."

Use *A Family Survival Kit* at your own pace, to meet your own current needs. Don't expect, or even try, to complete all the worksheets in a short period of time. We do suggest, however, that you begin with the first chapter, Keeping Family Records and Documents. Those worksheets are easily completed, and you'll be glad to have that information immediately. Then complete the chapters that are most important to you. You may want to get right to the analysis of your health insurance in Chapters 12 and 13, Serious Illness and Disability, for example, and leave Chapter 3, Figuring Your Net Worth, for last. Or jump straight to the last chapter, When a Death Occurs, and leave Borrowing, Chapter 5, for a rainy day.

The next time you're quizzed on your family's business, you'll have all the answers. You provided them.

I

BASIC
SURVIVAL
SAVVY

KEEPING FAMILY RECORDS AND DOCUMENTS

1

Some people keep them in shoe boxes, some people file them neatly in folders, and a lot of people stuff them into desk drawers. Everybody has a different way of dealing with family records, but what they all have in common is the desperate hope that when they need an important document, they can find it.

Sometimes you're lucky, but luck is a pretty slim reed to lean on when you're talking about your family's most important papers.

We have a neighbor who runs mostly on luck. It usually holds out—but not always. Every year before he goes off on vacation, he makes his Annual Passport Search. One year he found it in his golf bag (he'd been golfing in Scotland the previous summer), and one year he found it with his camera gear. Last year he couldn't find it for days, and even laid-back Tom was beginning to get a little frantic. But at the last minute it turned up—in his desk drawer. When he opened it, he saw that it had expired two months earlier.

Being organized, however, doesn't carry any guarantee, as Kathy, a young Kansas teacher, found out to her dismay. Kathy is married to a man who likes to handle all the family business on his own. Dan pays the bills and keeps track of the family papers. Kathy never thought about the arrangement—until Dan had a heart attack.

"It was a mess," said Kathy as she recalled the first days of her husband's illness. "Dan was in intensive care and I had to get into the safe-deposit box. Dan's secretary finally found the key, but the bank wouldn't let me open the box. They said I didn't have legal access to it."

Dan prided himself on his organization, but he was the only one who knew where everything was. Thinking he was safeguarding their important documents, for example, Dan kept them neatly in the safe-deposit box. "He never realized that no one else in the family knew where the key was, and couldn't use it anyway," said Kathy.

This time, Dan and Kathy were lucky. Although Dan was hooked up to heart-monitoring equipment, he could still sign his name on the bank's signature card and give other people access to the safe-deposit box.

Sam is a dentist we know who also keeps his records carefully filed. When the Internal Revenue Service notified him of an audit, Sam said, "My heart started to pound, but at least I didn't have the added anxiety of wondering where my records were." All his canceled checks and receipts were neatly filed, going back the requisite seven years.

Most people aren't as organized as Sam and Dan. They have important papers scattered all over—in bureau drawers at home, in office files, at a lawyer's, at a parent's house—and, like our neighbor, all too often they don't remember where the different documents are. Not only are these people disorganized, but they have put irreplaceable records in jeopardy.

The problem with important papers is you never know when you'll need them. Your family documents are required for any number of reasons that would never occur to you. After women get married, for instance, they have to produce their birth certificates, in order to change their drivers' licenses to their married names. When our daughter Samantha was eight and proudly opened her first bank account, she was surprised to learn she had to supply her Social Security number, along with her hard-earned savings.

Every family needs a system of maintaining records. Whether you're going overseas and need your passport, receive an unwelcome query from the Internal Revenue Service about a previous tax return, are moving to a new house, or selling a stock, you want to be able to put your hands on a document when you need it. What's more, we know you don't want to drown in paper; you want to keep just what you need, for as long as you need it, and no longer.

That's why we've worked out a detailed explanation of what important documents and records you should keep, where you should keep them, and for how long. Then we keyed this information to a series of worksheets on which to record this information for your family. As you'll see, together they give you a foolproof system for keeping records. The worksheets alone form a summary of your family's business that you'll find useful in many circumstances, and invaluable in an emergency.

YOUR IMPORTANT PAPERS AND WHERE TO KEEP THEM

There are many documents you should keep permanently, but there are others you only need for short periods. Some are safest in a bank vault. Others should never be kept in a safe-deposit box, in case it's sealed at the time of a death. In this chapter you'll learn where and how long to safeguard your documents.

You can keep your papers in a variety of places: a home file, in the office, or with your attorney, accountant, financial planner, tax consultant, or other close advisor. If records are difficult to replace, keep them in a safe-deposit box or in a fire-resistant container at home. Use only an insulated steel box that is labeled "fire resistant" and guaranteed to protect the contents against fire for at least one hour.

If we don't suggest a place to keep a particular document, you can keep it anywhere—just be sure other family members and/or friends know where that is. The best way to keep them informed is to give each a copy of the first worksheet, *Location of Important Papers*, which lists all your family documents and where they can be found.

Personal Documents

Certificates of birth. If you don't have birth certificates for every member of your family, take the time to get them now. They're needed for many things, from passport applications to the completion of death certificates.

For a nominal fee you can obtain copies of birth certificates in person or by mail from the County Hall of Records where the individual was born.

Be sure each copy is certified, that is, stamped with the official seal. An improperly validated birth certificate, or a copy of valid birth certificate without an original seal, is not acceptable in most instances. Keep all birth certificates in your safe-deposit box, permanently.

Certificates of marriage and divorce. These documents never seem important at the time, but when you change your name on a checking account, a Social Security card, or a driver's license, for instance, you may need to show one or both.

Request marriage and divorce certificates, stamped with the official seal, from the County Hall of Records where you were married or divorced. Get your marriage certificate from the Marriage Records division and your divorce certificate from the County Clerk where the divorce was filed. There is a small fee for each copy. Keep them in your safe-deposit box, permanently.

Social Security cards. Social Security numbers were once used primarily to enter the work force, but today they are required identification for many reasons that have nothing to do with employment.

Get a Social Security card for every member of your family, even newborn children and grandchildren. When you apply for one at your local Social Security office, bring your birth certificate and, if you're married, your marriage certificate.

Children under five need an additional piece of identification. It can be a baptismal certificate, an immunization record, or other medical card that proves the child exists. Children over five can use a school ID card or report card as additional identification.

Keep your Social Security card in your wallet, and the stub in your home file or safe-deposit box, permanently.

For a woman to change her Social Security card from her previous married name to her maiden name, she needs a certified copy of her divorce decree and one piece of identification. To change her Social Security card to her married name, she needs a marriage certificate and identification in her maiden name. If she prefers, she can have two surnames on her card, such as Smith-Jones.

If either of you lose your Social Security card, you need your birth certificate plus two pieces of identification to get a replacement.

Military discharge papers. You may not ever need (or want) to look at these papers again, but, on the other hand, you may have to prove the length and status of your military service to claim government disability payments, qualify for a real estate tax exemption, get a particular loan, run for public office, or be buried in Arlington National Cemetery.

If you misplace your original papers, request duplicates by writing to the branch of the military from which you were discharged. Keep your discharge papers in a safe-deposit box, permanently.

Passports. If you like to be prepared for an overseas trip at a moment's notice, you'll want to have a valid passport at the ready. At peak travel times, it often takes two to three weeks to get one.

You can get a passport application at your local post office, and mail it to a nearby federal passport office. (First-time applicants need a birth certificate or U.S. naturalization papers and two passport photographs.) If you're pressed for time, you can apply in person. Passport offices are listed in the phone book under "Federal" or, sometimes, "County Offices." Passports are now good for ten years (five for minors) and are easily renewed with a currently valid passport. Keep valid passports in your safe-deposit box or home file.

Wills. If you haven't yet drawn a will, read Chapter 9, Distributing Your Assets. Promptly.

We suggest that you give your attorney the original copy of your will, retaining only a copy of it for yourself. Never place the original in your safe-deposit box. If you write a new will, you should destroy the old one; this erases any doubts that the new will wasn't intended to replace the old one. And if a different attorney draws the new will, ask the previous lawyer to destroy the old will and/or any copies he holds.

Death certificate. A certificate of death is issued by the county registrar and signed by a doctor. After someone dies, make a written request for at least twenty certified copies of the certificate of death from the county registrar; you'll have to produce them for a multitude of reasons, from changing charge accounts and collecting Social Security benefits to making life insurance claims and filing final state and federal income tax returns. Remember to keep one copy permanently in your safe-deposit box.

If death occurs in a foreign country, contact the American Embassy.

Financial Documents

Bank account information. Keep all bank statements, canceled checks, loan payments, and credit card statements that were used in filing income tax returns for seven years. You don't need to keep canceled checks, credit card statements, and other financial records that don't document income tax returns for more than one year. Record all bank account information on the *Banking Information (#2)* worksheet at the end of the book.

Copies of loan agreements. Always keep a copy of any loan agreement that is currently in force. For income tax purposes, keep copies of previous, paid-off loans for seven years.

Stocks, bonds, and government securities. When you want to sell stocks or bonds, place them as security for a loan, or settle an estate, you'll need the actual certificates. Because they are difficult and time-consuming to replace, keep them in a safe place, like your safe-deposit box. You can also leave them with your bank or stockbroker if they offer safekeeping services. Regardless of where you keep the actual certificates, list your holdings on the *List of Stock Securities (#3)* and *List of Bond Securities (#4)* worksheets found in the Workbook section of this book, and keep them up to date.

Passbooks. Keep information in your safe-deposit box as long as an account is open.

Pension and profit-sharing plans. Normally your employer will give you an annual record of your pension and profit-sharing plan. Keep this in a special file in your safe-deposit box as a permanent record of your account. If you have an Individual Retirement Account (IRA) and/or Keogh Plan, keep these in the same place.

Taxes

The Internal Revenue Service recommends that you keep copies of your income tax returns and the canceled checks that apply to those returns for at least seven years. The seven-year period is the statute of limitations for returns that understate income by more than the allowable limit.

Insurance Records

Keep all of your insurance policies in the same place—and contrary to popular belief, that doesn't have to be your safe-deposit box. In fact, you specifically wouldn't want your life insurance policies there in case the box is sealed in the event of a death. Both your insurance agent and the insurance company have copies of all your policies, so if you've misplaced yours, ask them for a certified copy.

Keep an up-to-date record of your insurance on the *Current Insurance Policies (#5)* worksheet.

Real Estate

With real estate, the best rule is to keep everything—certainly everything related to property you own. That would include trust deeds, real estate notes, title policy, and mortgage documents. You should also keep a file of receipts for capital improvements. When you sell the improved property, those receipted amounts may reduce your capital gain and provide a tax reduction.

Record all your holdings on the *Real Estate Properties* (#6) worksheet.

If you rent, you don't need to keep rental agreements and rent receipts for more than three years.

Medical Documents

Medical records. Keep records of immunizations, booster shots, and information on all major illnesses and surgery for every member of your family. As a precaution, also note everybody's blood type and any food or drug allergies.

Medical receipts. These include bills and canceled checks for doctors, dentists, nurses, physical therapists, hospitals, laboratories, pharmacies, nursing homes, eyeglasses, and medical insurance, as well as transportation costs for medical treatments. Since these document your medical deductions on your income tax report, keep them for seven years for possible tax audits. If any medical care is the result of an accident or negligence by others, keep all receipts in case of litigation, or until the case is settled.

Autos

The registration and certificate of title proving your ownership are extremely important. Without them you'll have difficulty selling or trading your car. Keep the original certificate of title in your safe-deposit box—*not* in your car.

Divide the registration into its two parts, and keep the renewal half at home and the other half in the car. In most states it is illegal to drive with a copy of the registration; you must have the original.

Keep the car loan agreement and records of the loan payments for three years. If you lease a car, keep the agreement for the length of the lease. Retain car repair receipts for three years; they would be invaluable if you wanted to sue because of an accident or needed to defend yourself if someone else is injured due to mechanical failure of your car.

Safe-Deposit Box

It's crucial that members of your family know in which bank you have a safe-deposit box and where you keep the keys to it. You'll probably receive two keys.

On the *Safe-Deposit Box Information and Contents* (#7) worksheet, be sure to list where you keep both keys. You might keep one at home and one in the office, but don't keep both of them in the same place.

Also, list the people who have access to the box. Be sure those names are filed with the bank on valid bank signature cards and also that those individuals know they are authorized to get into the box.

You might want to consider forming a family corporation and renting a safe-deposit box in your family name. That way your safe-deposit box can't be sealed on the death of one of the principals; members of the family will have continuing access to the box, and you can keep whatever you want in it.

Power of Attorney

A power of attorney is an agreement that gives one individual the right to act on behalf of another. You can name someone to act for you in all circumstances, or just in specific situations. When you describe the power of attorney on the *Location of Important Papers* (#1) worksheet, name the people who hold your power of attorney and describe the limits, if any.

Powers of attorney are usually revoked after the death of the individual.

FAMILY STATUS

The *Family Status Record* (#8) worksheet holds all your family's vital statistics. Remember to update the information at every birth, death, marriage, or divorce in your family so the record is always current.

BANKING INFORMATION

The *Banking Information* (#2) worksheet provides a complete list of your bank account information. Be sure to note whose name each account is in—joint, husband, or wife—and whether it's in trust for someone.

MARKETABLE SECURITIES

Here's where you record all pertinent data about your securities, either on the *List of Stock Securities* (#3) or *List of Bond Securities* (#4) worksheets. Include government securities with the bonds. Remember to keep these worksheets current, and record all buy-and-sell transactions.

NOTES

The *Notes Information* (#9) worksheet lists the pertinent data about all notes due you or due others.

CURRENT INSURANCE POLICIES

This is the master list of your family's insurance. Although details of each type of insurance are given in succeeding chapters, keep this overall record up to date on the *Current Insurance Policies* (#5) worksheet.

LIST OF CREDIT CARDS

Credit card fraud is increasing, and not only from lost or stolen cards. Counterfeiters are manufacturing phony cards that can utilize your valid credit card number while the actual card is still in your pocket. It's increasingly important to keep a list of all your credit cards so you can notify the various credit card companies as soon as you miss a card or are charged for purchases you didn't make.

Use the *List of Credit Cards* (#10) worksheet, updating it every time you get a new, or renewed, card. Also note who else is authorized to use each card.

IMPORTANT ADVISORS

Knowing who handles your personal and business affairs is obviously important to your family, so give each person who should have that information a copy of the *List of Important Advisors* (#11) worksheet. It's also helpful to send a copy to each of your advisors so they'll know who the others are and how to contact them.

SURVIVAL KIT SAVVY

When you've completed these worksheets, you've made a terrific start on organizing your family records. But if the two of you are the only ones who know where everything is, it won't help your family in an emergency. It's essential to alert your family to the worksheets in this book, and particularly to the *Location of Important Papers* (#1) worksheet.

We believe every adult member of your family should know exactly where you keep your important documents, and that you've provided a complete inventory of them. The way to do this is to give each of them a copy of the *Location of Important Papers* (#1) worksheet. If you have young children and no other family nearby, alert a close friend to the existence of this worksheet and where you keep it. And, of course, give a copy to your lawyer.

Once you've completed the worksheets, you've done the hard work. Remember to update these forms at least once a year, and send the current copies to your attorney. The continuing value of this book is in your hands.

PICKING YOUR ADVISORY TEAM

2

"There's so much you take for granted when you're married," sighed Tom, an English professor who was widowed two years ago. "I'm talking about things like deciding whether to buy a stock or increase your insurance." Tom's wife headed a financial consulting firm, and her advice was critical.

"Boy, is that true," agreed Julie, a family counselor whose husband died seven years ago. "Take doing your income tax. All of a sudden there's no one around to help you."

A few of us were sitting around, discussing how hard it is to take on all the family decisions by yourself, especially if you've never made them before. Tom's and Julie's stories were so typical of the men and women with whom we talked they were almost textbook cases.

Like many people who are widowed or divorced, Tom and Julie were overwhelmed by all the financial and family details that their spouses had handled. Now they had to take care of everything themselves—including dealing with attorneys, accountants, and financial advisors—just at the time they were emotionally least able to cope.

Tom's problems started right after Joy died when he turned to their lawyer, who was also a family friend.

"Naturally I expected him to settle the estate," Tom said. "And he refused. He was very nice about it, but he said he was also the lawyer for Joy's business, and there would be a conflict of interest. His obligation was to represent the company and not me. He told me I'd have to find another lawyer. I felt betrayed," said Tom.

Julie had a similar problem, which was complicated because her husband had a business partner. A friend recommended an accountant, but Julie felt he didn't pay enough attention to her affairs. For him it was a small estate. For her it was everything. "The chemistry just wasn't good," she said.

"But the worst part," Julie recalled, "was having to sit in an office with a male attorney, a male accountant, and a male business partner—and their attitude was I didn't know a damn thing, leave it to them."

The memory still infuriates Julie, and it made her almost evangelical about people understanding their business affairs. "If you have the information, and the professionals see you know what you're talking about, they're going to treat you with more respect," she said. It's advice she gives to everyone who comes to her for counseling.

As if settling an estate isn't traumatic enough, financial advisors suddenly popped up everywhere. "Everybody is after you, no matter what your income is," said Julie. "I got hit by every charlatan in town after Rob died. People wanted to sell me all kinds of things, and they sounded wonderful. They think you've got some money and you don't know much—and they're right. It's overwhelming if you've never had to manage money before."

Many newly single people have no idea what they can afford to do, and what they can't. Others turn their assets over to money managers without checking credentials. Some are lucky, some aren't.

One of the unlucky ones told us, "You sort of fumble and bumble around, and how do you know whether the financial advice is good, bad, or indifferent? It makes a lot of difference, it makes a hell of a lot of difference."

When you're widowed or divorced, your need for advice is sudden and acute. "No matter how self-sufficient you think you are, you feel lost and vulnerable," said Tom. "More than anything you just want somebody you can rely on who's going to take care of things for you."

There are many fine, well-qualified professionals who will take your best interests to heart, and there are those who won't. Sometimes it's hard to tell the difference. We'll tell you how to make that important distinction in this chapter.

What's important is to pick *your* team of professionals—*your* lawyer, accountant, insurance agent, stockbroker, or investment advisor. You may want to continue with all your regular family advisors, or you may want to change one or more of them. Don't use any advisor you aren't comfortable with.

EVALUATING PROSPECTIVE ADVISORS

If you want to make changes in this advisory team, or select new advisors, keep the following guidelines in mind:

- Choose advisors who work full time in their professions.
- Favor people who have attained professional designations in their fields

by passing proficiency exams. A title doesn't guarantee superiority, but it does indicate effort and study in the field.

- Be wary of using friends and relatives. Will you replace them if they don't perform satisfactorily? Would you choose them if they didn't have a special relationship with you? Are they complacent about their responsibilities because of their relationship?
- Select your advisors based on the clients they represent, particularly if they are people whom you respect.

Don't be reluctant to question potential advisors. The best way to see if they are right for you is to interview each one. You'll want to know their professional credentials and experience, and how their office functions. To help your search, you'll find two worksheets—*Interview Questions for Prospective Advisors* (#12) and *Advisor Evaluation Guide* (#13)—in the Workbook section of this book. Take them with you when you interview advisors.

Rate potential advisors on your feelings about them after your initial visit. For example:

How quickly do they return your telephone calls?

Do they treat your professional needs with respect?

Do you think they'll give you adequate attention?

Are you more comfortable with a large or small firm?

What is your gut feeling about them?

Advisors and Their Fees

When picking advisors, don't base your choice on their fees. First select professionals who seem most competent and with whom you feel at ease. Consider their fees last. In some instances, fees may be negotiable. And if you think the fees are out of line, discuss that with them directly. Sometimes it's in your best interest to pay more for better advice and services.

If a potential advisor offers to counsel you gratis, out of friendship for your family or a special relationship, reject the offer graciously. The principal advantage of paying your advisors a fee for their efforts is that you can change advisors when you feel it's necessary. And don't hesitate to do that if you feel you've made the wrong choice.

Also, in time, your own needs may change, and the reasons why you selected the advisor may no longer apply. You'll be glad to be free to rethink your needs and pick new advisors who fit your current requirements.

In all major decisions—and picking your advisory team is surely one— get as much advice as possible. The person who becomes a financial wizard by making rapid decisions is a storybook stereotype, a fantasy; smart and prudent people seek advice widely before making important decisions.

When you've chosen your advisors, add them to the *List of Important Advisors* (#11) worksheet in the Workbook section.

SELECTING AN ATTORNEY

When a wife inherits her husband's attorney, she is likely to run into problems. As Julie discovered, conflict of interest is a common one. In fact, in new circumstances, widows and divorcées often need altogether different legal counsel than they had before.

Whether you need an estate lawyer, a bankruptcy lawyer, or another specialist, try to select an attorney or law firm that specializes in the field in which your problem exists. A good corporate attorney may not be a good tax or divorce lawyer.

Locating Lawyers

You can find the names of attorneys to interview from several sources:

- Referrals from friends who have had good experiences.
- Martindale-Hubbell publishes and regularly updates a book that describes all law firms and rates some. Consult it at your local library or in the office of a friendly attorney.
- The local bar association; area law schools, which normally have a referral service; and lawyer referral services, often listed in the classified pages of your telephone directory.
- The local office of the National Organization of Women (NOW), which normally refers women attorneys.
- Your accountant or banker.

If you decide not to use a private attorney, you can get legal help from special organizations. For example, Legal Action Workshop is a national organization of attorneys who can counsel you at their various offices. They specialize in relatively short interviews and immediate advice rather than long-term client relationships. They also offer prerecorded tapes about specific legal problems such as simple consumer suits or divorce.

SELECTING AN ACCOUNTANT

If you think of your accountant as someone who only prepares tax returns, either you aren't utilizing your accountant's full talents or you have the wrong consultant. Your accountant should be not only your financial caretaker, but also your financial advisor.

Sometimes the financial needs of husbands and wives are not the same, which is most often the case when settling an estate. For instance, after her husband died, Julie was caught in a complicated dispute with her husband's partner. "Rob's partner wanted us to use the firm accountant to go over the records of the business, and that just didn't sit right with me," she said.

Julie's instincts were right. Even if you have a good relationship with your accountant, there are many situations, especially in settling estates, when you'll be better served by an accountant who has no prior association with your family business. Don't hesitate to call in an independent CPA and really challenge what is going on.

There are several types of accountants, and in selecting an advisor, it's helpful to understand the field. Like an attorney, an accountant can be a general practitioner or a specialist in business affairs, tax matters, or financial investments. The highest designation in the field is a Certified Public Accountant (CPA). To become a CPA, an accountant must pass a national examination given by the American Institute of Certified Public Accountants and work for a public accounting firm for at least two years.

Public accountants (they are not *certified* public accountants) are now licensed in many states. Their only limitation is that they can't represent you with tax audits or in tax courts.

In selecting an accountant, first consider a CPA. His designation doesn't guarantee performance, but it's an indication of his seriousness and commitment, and he'll be able to handle all your financial needs.

Locating Accountants

You can find the names of accountants to interview from several good sources:

- Your local banker or attorney.
- Your state licensing or control board, which can certify the good standing of prospective accountants.
- Local and state associations of accountants for their referral services.
- If you don't require extensive experience, you can probably keep your costs to a minimum by calling an area university for the names of recent graduates in accounting.

Taxes, Taxes

You can get tax help from three types of professionals, depending on your needs:

1. *Tax Attorneys* frequently provide year-round tax planning and can represent you before the Internal Revenue Service if you are audited, and in a court of law to resolve tax disputes. Normally, they don't prepare tax returns, and aren't experienced in their preparation.
2. *Tax Accountants* prepare tax returns, normally provide year-round tax planning, and can represent you before the I.R.S. if you are audited.
3. *Enrolled Agents* also prepare tax returns, provide year-round tax planning, and can represent you before the I.R.S. They are proficient in tax matters but they are not accountants. They normally charge less than a tax attorney or accountant, and often advertise heavily just prior to April 15.

If you have your tax returns prepared by someone who is not your regular accountant, be sure you get the following information:

- Does the tax preparer belong to a professional association?
- Will this individual be around after April 15, in case questions arise about your tax return or you are audited? (An audit can occur anytime up to three years after you filed a tax return.) If this person is at a temporary location, get a permanent telephone number for future contact.
- Before you start, get an estimate in writing of the cost of your tax return preparation. If you are refused, you may want to reconsider doing business with that individual.
- Will the tax preparer pay your fees if his error leads to an audit, and any penalties and/or interest resulting from that audit? You'd be wise to get that commitment in writing.

Regardless who prepares your tax returns, try to have some continuity in tax advisors. In case the Internal Revenue Service audits more than one year's return, you'll be better served if one person or firm has been handling you for each of those years.

The Internal Revenue Service gives advice—by phone or at their offices—on tax matters. It also offers a number of publications about taxes.

SELECTING AN INSURANCE AGENT OR INSURANCE BROKER

Some people make a distinction between an insurance agent and an insurance broker. An agent can represent one or more insurance companies and can bind insurance coverage on their behalf; a broker represents the client and normally can't bind coverage for a specific insurance company. Most agents and brokers hold both licenses, and the distinction is minimal.

For both agent and broker licenses, the highest designations are Certified Life Underwriter (CLU) for the life and health insurance agent, and Chartered Property and Casualty Underwriter (CPCU) for the automobile and homeowner's insurance agent.

We suggest that you select one person to handle your life and disability insurance, and another for your automobile and homeowner's insurance. It's difficult for one person to be knowledgeable in both areas.

Deal with a professional who has been in business for a reasonable period of time. The turnover in this field, particularly in life insurance, is extremely high, and you want an experienced agent or broker who intends to remain in the business.

Locating Insurance Agents and Brokers

Some sources for names of agents and brokers in your area include:

- National Association of Life Underwriters, 1922 F Street, N.W., Washington, D.C. 20006.
- One of the local life insurance agents' associations in your area.
- The Independent Insurance Agents Association of America, 100 Church Street, New York, NY 10008.

- The National Association of Casualty and Surety Agents, 5454 Wisconsin Avenue, Chevy Chase, MD 20815.
- The local independent agents' association for property and casualty insurance in your area.
- The offices of any major insurance company.

After you've narrowed your choice to one or more prospective agents or brokers, you can contact your state insurance department to find out if those individuals are in good standing.

SELECTING A STOCKBROKER

If you have money to invest, the choice of a stockbroker or investment advisor is everything. It's particularly confusing these days because both of them now do practically the same things. Stockbrokers buy and sell securities, and may also sell life insurance or real estate syndicated partnerships. So do investment advisors. Brokers are paid by commission on each sale; investment advisors usually charge an additional fee, often a percentage of the total value of your investment portfolio.

With the vast and rapid changes occurring in the financial advisor field, it's hard to predict precisely who will perform what function. What's most important is to choose an advisor who has not recently converted from another area to this field. Find out how long your prospective money handlers have actively practiced their specialties, then check with a few of their clients about their ability to handle your specific needs.

The Security and Exchange Commission (SEC) oversees all of a broker's actions except his competence. You have to judge that.

The best test of any advisor is his performance record. And the best way to measure that is to talk with long-standing customers. You can also query a prospective broker or investment advisor directly about his investment record. He may be able to document it with a fund his firm administers.

We recommend that you only consider brokers who have been with their firms for at least a year. There is high turnover in this field, and the longer a broker has been in business, the safer your investments will be.

If you have any questions about the standing of particular brokers, query the Security and Exchange Commission, 500 North Capital Street, N.W., Washington, D.C. 20549.

The best way to select a financial advisor is to arm yourself with as much information as possible. Take financial planning courses at local universities or adult education schools. Book an hour's consultation with an investment counselor (many offer a free consultation hour).

II

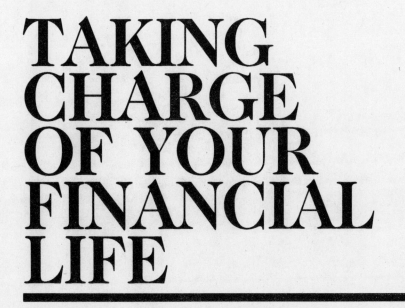

TAKING CHARGE OF YOUR FINANCIAL LIFE

FIGURING YOUR NET WORTH

3

Do you know how much you're worth?

You might think that's an idle question since you're probably not up for inclusion in the list of the "Ten Richest People in the World." But you'd be surprised how often you need that information—and how few people have it at hand.

Nan is one of them. Like many women, she turned a homegrown talent into a thriving business. Egged on by everyone who tasted her incredible lemon cake and triple chocolate walnut torte, she launched Nan's Fancies with a cake and coffee buffet, and a toast to America's sweet tooth.

Now she turned away from the large ovens, wiped floury hands on her apron, and pointed to the commercial kitchen in the shopping center storefront. "Do you know how much this cost?" she asked. "I couldn't have swung it without a loan.

"I'd always left family finances to Bill," she said, "but this was my own business and I wanted to do it myself." After all her careful research into health codes, packaging, marketing, and profit margins, Nan hadn't expected to stumble at her first stop, the bank.

"When I went in for the loan, and the bank officer asked for my net worth," said Nan, "I didn't know what he meant."

Except for the details, our friend Sam told a similar tale. "My rental apartment was going co-op, and the insider's price was too good to pass up," he said. "The loan broker told me to bring in my financial statement." Financial statement? Sam is an editor; to him, financial statements mean how many books were sold, and at what price.

"It turned out they wanted to know everything I own, and everything I owe!" Sam's eyes roll as he remembers the scene. "It was some mess getting it together in a hurry."

Actually, we know just how Sam felt. We recently had to prepare the same kind of financial statement when we wanted to consult a particular financial advisor whose clients must have a minimum net worth.

Whether you're borrowing money to start a business, buying a house or apartment, or just want to find out how much you're worth, eventually you'll have to complete a financial statement. This simply states what you are worth. It's a fairly standard document, but it looks complicated and imposing, full of terms that you may not find familiar or even understandable. Just the sight of it makes most of us throw up our hands in despair.

To help you tackle the unfamiliar, we've defined all the items that make up net worth. We've also included two worksheets for you to fill in with your own information: *Record of Assets* (#14) and *Record of Liabilities* (#15). This is the same information financial institutions request, and in most cases, you can submit it on these worksheets. If you can't, you can easily adapt them to the institution's forms.

Think of your net worth statement as a snapshot giving you a picture of your financial position as of a certain date. You don't have to write down the information on the same day, but it should all refer to the same *specific date*. Recording information about earlier or later dates can blur your financial picture. Even if you complete these worksheets well after your chosen Net Worth Date, use information and bank statements that are closest to that date rather than current information. Pick a date to use for all your financial information. Most people choose the end of a month, say March 31, or the end of a fiscal reporting period, for example, December 31. Always designate your net worth with that date, and record it as "Net Worth, as of (date and year)."

Evaluate each item, based on your total liability, as of your Net Worth Date. On a loan, for instance, figure what you owe as of your Net Worth Date, not the original amount of the loan. On such long-term commitments as rent, calculate the remainder of your lease.

If you compute your assets and liabilities at your own pace, completing the two worksheets won't be as burdensome as it may now appear. Besides, you'll find the answer to that mystery at the bottom line: What am I worth?

YOUR ASSETS

In a financial statement, your assets are defined as everything you own that has a cash value.

Cash

Cash includes the money you currently have on hand, in currency and travelers checks, as of the Net Worth Date. It also reflects your bank balances as of that date. For example, if you pick December 31 as your Net Worth Date, record the balance in your checking, savings, and bank money market accounts as of December 31. You'll get those statements in January.

Securities

These include money market funds, stocks, bonds, and mutual funds.

Money market funds. Record their value as of your selected date, using your money market statement.

Stocks. To compute the value of your stocks as of the Net Worth Date, check their value in the financial pages of your local newspaper on the evening of that date or in the next morning's financial pages. You'll find them in the New York Stock Exchange, American Stock Exchange, or over-the-counter market listings. If necessary, your stockbroker can help you with this information.

Bonds. To figure the value of municipal or U.S. Savings Bonds, list them at their current value—not their anticipated value at maturity. Any bank can compute the figure for your savings bonds.

Mutual funds. Record the value of your mutual funds as shown on the mutual fund statement covering your Net Worth Date.

Other Investments

If you have invested in certificates of deposit (CDs), compute their worth on the initial investments as of the Net Worth Date. Don't record the total anticipated interest because you may cash in the certificate before it matures, thereby forfeiting some or all of the accrued interest. For bank repurchase agreements, list the face amount of the investment, and don't include the potential interest.

Life Insurance

All whole or straight life insurance policies have a cash surrender value. That's the amount you would receive if you were to cash in the insurance on a particular date. You can determine this amount by checking the cash surrender value chart on each policy and computing its value as of your Net Worth Date. Be sure to deduct any outstanding loan you have against the policy. If in doubt about the exact figure, ask your agent or the life insurance company.

Notes Receivable

This is bank talk for money you have loaned to others that you're fairly certain will be repaid. Don't count outright gifts or bad loans.

Real Estate

You can get an estimate of the value of your real estate holdings from a local real estate broker, or a formal property appraisal from a real estate appraiser. Most banks can provide you with the names of several real estate appraisers.

If your property is mortgaged, the mortgage holder may have a recent appraisal and can supply its current value.

Autos and Other Vehicles

The current value of your cars, trucks, campers, and other vehicles is listed in the *Kelly Blue Book*. You can find it at banks, automobile dealers, and auto clubs.

Pension and/or Profit-Sharing Plans

Your current employer will know the value and status of your participation in the pension and/or profit-sharing plans. Ask him to evaluate your share as of your Net Worth Date.

If you invested in a pension and/or profit-sharing plan with a previous employer, and if any of those funds were not paid out to you when you left that job, add them to your present pension plan.

Keogh and/or Individual Retirement Accounts (IRA)

Your latest statements on those accounts will give you their value. If your selected Net Worth Date is not within the current month, use a previous statement.

Other Assets

This is a catch-all for any property, other than real estate, that has cash value. It includes your home furnishings and household goods, jewelry, furs, antiques, art, collectibles, and anything else you think has value.

It's difficult to place dollar values on some of these assets, since we tend to focus on what we originally paid for an item rather than its current depreciated (or appreciated) worth. As a general rule of thumb, you can evaluate the total personal property in your home at 40 percent (or less) of the value of the home itself. This is the figure generally used by insurance companies for household goods insured under a homeowner's insurance policy.

You may want to determine the value of specific items. Jewelry, furs, antiques, art, silver, and collectibles can be appraised by competent appraisers who will visit your home, if requested. Appraisers charge varying fees, sometimes based on the value of the property, their time, or sometimes a flat fee, so get several estimates. Your household insurance agent can usually provide names of appraisers.

The information and worksheets in Chapter 14, Property Loss and Other Accidents, will be helpful.

YOUR LIABILITIES

In a financial statement, liabilities refer to your debts. They include everything you owe.

Accounts Payable

This is money you owe others, such as bills you haven't yet paid. These would be purchases made on charge cards, credit cards, and charge accounts. They also include medical bills, utility bills, lease payments, alimony, and child support payments. The most accurate way to tally these liabilities is to figure what you are legally obligated to pay over the next twelve months.

For charge cards, credit cards, and charge accounts, record the total amount you owe, even if you may not be planning to pay it all in your next payment.

Report all other accounts payable from the actual unpaid bills you have on hand as of your Net Worth Date. Also, record other bills you have recently incurred but have not yet received as of your Net Worth Date.

Loans Payable

Contracts payable.   This is financial talk for loans secured by an item such as a car or furniture; it is money you owe others under a formal contract. It includes payments for automobiles, furniture, and other installment credit obligations. It does not include bank loans or real estate mortgages, which are reported in the following category of Notes Payable to Others.

If you aren't sure of the current balance of any contracts payable (loans), contact the lender for up-to-date information.

Notes payable to others.   These are normally loans based on your good credit. They include bank loans, real estate mortgages, and other notes, such as loans from credit unions, profit-sharing plans, or emergency loans from your pension plan.

With both contracts and notes payable, report your entire debt, including principal and total interest, as well as the total remaining balance on the loan (not just the installment due on your current statement).

Taxes

The taxes you owe—property taxes, and federal and state income taxes—are also liabilities. To figure your true net worth, report all taxes that you owe but have not yet paid for the current year.

To figure all property taxes, call the tax assessor's office for your municipality. If you have already paid any portion of your property taxes for the year—either directly or to a monthly escrow account with your mortgage holder—deduct those payments from your total annual property tax bill.

To record your state and federal income taxes, consult your last year's income tax return or your estimated income tax return for the current year. Your accountant can give you those figures as well as his estimate of your current taxes. Again, deduct from the total any payments you have already made for the current year, including taxes withheld by your employer.

YOUR NET WORTH

You net worth is everything you own minus your debts. To determine it, just subtract your total liabilities from your total assets.

It's a good idea to compute your net worth annually. You'll find it useful in securing bank loans, in making up household budgets, and in evaluating your assets for a disability plan. You'll see how your assets and liabilities are distributed, and with annual evaluations, you can track the growth of your family's worth.

BANKING

4

"When I was young, I put my savings in a savings bank, and paid my bills from a checking account," said Janet, the office manager for a law firm in Houston. "After I started working, my husband, Al, suggested I open my own bank account. All I knew was I wanted a bank with an automated teller so I could get money anytime. Beyond that, there were so many possibilities and choices I didn't have the faintest idea where to go."

Most of us remember the simplicity of the good old days when you put your birthday check in a savings bank, got a mortgage from a savings and loan, a personal loan from the credit union, and bought securities from your broker. But managing money is a lot more complicated now.

"I didn't know if I should have a regular checking account or one of those special accounts," she said. "Or one of those money market funds that are at brokerage houses and now at banks. And I certainly didn't know the difference among them, anyway."

Vivian is a thirty-four-year-old schoolteacher we met in Chicago who had a different problem. She needed financial advice, and didn't realize that the good old-fashioned trust department of her bank could help. "I always thought trust departments were for widows or orphans," she said, "but nothing could be further from the truth. I discovered that by chance at the bank when I went in for some tax forms for my mother."

Vivian shook her head as she recounted her mother's predicament. "She doesn't have much financial expertise, and all of a sudden she had to make year-end financial decisions involving substantial funds. My father used to do all that, but his Parkinson's disease is getting worse, and now my grand-mother is senile, so there's her estate, too."

At sixty-five, Vivian's mother is swamped by the emotional toll of a dying husband and a senile mother and these new financial burdens. She turned to Vivian, who didn't have the faintest idea what to do, until her chance conversation at the bank.

No wonder Janet and Vivian were confused. In the last few years, banks, savings and loans, and stockbrokers have been able to expand their services so widely that they often do virtually the same things. Today, you can buy securities at your commercial bank and write checks against your investment broker's money market fund. And all of that sometimes obscures the traditional services that banks still perform, sometimes differently than they used to. Add to that the changing nature of financial institutions, and even professionals are hard put to keep current.

In this chapter we've sorted out the main banking services, and give some guidelines on how to find what you need.

HOW TO CHOOSE AMONG THEM

There are four main factors to consider when making your choice: services, convenience, safety, and contacts.

Services. Although most financial institutions offer similar services, there are often important differences among them. For example, commercial banks, known as full-service banks, offer deposit, payment, and credit functions to their customers. Public brokerage houses ("non-bank" banks) offer a host of services but not loans. If you have children in high school, you might want a bank that gives college loans; if you're planning for retirement, you'll be interested in a bank's Keogh and IRA capabilities.

Detailed descriptions of basic financial services follow later in this chapter. The *Banking Services Checklist* (#16) in the Workbook section at the end of the book lists all the services you are likely to want. Use it to determine which institutions meet your needs.

Convenience. If you live and work in a small community where it's not inconvenient to have a checking account in one bank, a savings account across the street, and a market account at the local stock brokerage house, or if you don't mind banking by mail, you can utilize several different institutions. If it's more convenient to bank under one roof, use the *Banking Services Checklist* (#16) to compare the services offered by large financial institutions.

If you require a wide range of banking services but have few investment needs, consider a full-service commercial bank. For example, Al does all the family investing but Janet often needs money orders for her mother, and traveler's checks for trips.

One aspect of convenience is how quickly you have access to your funds. How long does it take local, in-state, and out-of-state checks to clear? How fast can you draw against your deposits?

Another aspect is ease of doing business. What are the banking hours? Do they meet your needs? Is there an automated teller system? Can you bank by mail? Are there Saturday or extended banking hours? The *Banking Services Checklist* (#16) will help you assess your needs.

Safety. Whichever financial institutions you choose, make sure they are insured. In the United States, most banks are insured by the Federal Deposit Insurance Corp. (FDIC), and most federal and state-chartered savings and loan associations by the Federal Savings and Loan Insurance Corp. (FSLIC). This means that deposits in each account in one name in one bank are insured up to $100,000. Note that a joint account does not increase the insured amount. If a bank fails, depositors usually have to wait some time before receiving their money, so having your deposit insured doesn't altogether eliminate potential problems.

Funds held by new financial entities—such as savings and loans, money market funds, and investment brokers—may or may not be insured by state-controlled insurance programs. Make sure the institution you are dealing with is insured.

In addition to insurance, check the soundness of prospective institutions. "In this era of serious questions about the stability of financial institutions, a look at your bank's 'statement of condition' or annual stockholder report is a good idea," advises financial expert Grace W. Weinstein, author of *The Lifetime Book of Money Management*. She believes a bank's accessible funds should be more than 50 percent of deposits and its net worth at least 5 percent of its assets.

Contacts. Any financial institution that has an established personal or corporate relationship with you will most likely be happy to help you with your financial needs. If the bank has a major business relationship with you, it may waive some or all of its service charges and fees.

Making Contact

Even if you have no special entrée to a bank, you'll get better service if you approach them in a businesslike way. Many people simply stop at the desk that has the sign "New Accounts." We think that's a mistake, though you could say to the person there: "I'd like to talk to someone who can discuss all the options your bank offers. Who could spend fifteen or twenty minutes with me to do that?"

Chances are you'll be directed to an officer of the bank or the branch manager. Officers and managers don't deal exclusively with corporations. They want to talk to people in the community. They'll steer you to the most knowledgeable people in the bank for your particular needs, whether it's opening an account, trust or loan information, or anything else.

The banking worksheets (#s 16–19) will help you evaluate competing institutions, their services, and their personnel. Clip them out of the Workbook section and take them with you as you interview various financial institutions.

BANK ACCOUNTS

Checking Accounts

Regular checking accounts.   These allow you to write an unlimited number of checks each month. If you maintain a minimum balance at all times, most banks provide free checking; otherwise, the service fee is minimal. Conventional accounts pay no or low interest on your balance.

Interest-bearing checking account.   Most banks provide free unlimited checking if you maintain a minimum balance (usually from $500 to $3,000) in this type of account. If your balance dips below the minimum, the bank levies a service fee that is usually minimal. An interest-bearing account pays low interest on the balance you maintain. Consider this if you write a large number of monthly checks and don't mind maintaining the required minimum balance.

Money market checking account (sometimes called a market rate account). If you want to have readily accessible cash that still earns high interest, consider a bank's money market checking account—it has a variety of names (Super Now is one of them). Its rates compete with the yield from money market mutual funds, but, unlike them, it is federally insured. The bank requires a minimum balance (usually $2,500), and if the balance falls below the minimum, it pays lower prevailing interest rates. You can only write three to five checks a month, although you can withdraw any amount of cash from the account at any time. If you write a lot of checks a month, open a regular or special checking account and replenish it from a money market checking account.

Money market mutual fund.   Technically, these funds are not bank accounts because they are managed by stock brokerage firms, not banks, but they offer many attractive features to compete with a bank's money market checking account. For the same liquidity, comparable or higher interest rates, you can write unlimited checks (some funds require a $250 or $500 minimum, others none at all). Initial deposits may range from no minimum to $250 to $2,500. The funds are not federally insured, although some are privately insured. Brokerage houses often offer several funds, with different features. For example, Merrill Lynch has six funds, including a Cash Management Account and Ready Assets. Most of these accounts are listed with their current rates in the *Wall Street Journal* and in the business section of most daily newspapers.

Savings Accounts

Passbook account.   All banks and savings and loans still offer the familiar passbook savings account. These return low interest, and don't offer any benefits. If you're loyal to a passbook account, at least be sure it compounds interest daily, from day of deposit to day of withdrawal.

Trust account.   You can open this type of account "in trust for" someone else (usually a child), who receives the money at your death. Meanwhile, you pay taxes on the interest, and you can change the beneficiary and close the account at any time.

Custodial account.   This is similar to a trust account except that the beneficiary pays taxes on the interest, presumably at a lower rate than you would pay, and is legally entitled to all the funds in the account; you can't change the beneficiary or close the account.

   If you're putting money aside for a child, say for college, a custodial account is useful for transferring assets out of your higher-taxed estate. As the custodian, you can invest a custodial account in a certificate of deposit rather than a lower-interest passbook savings account. (For other ways to transfer assets to your children, see Chapter 8, Planning Your Estate, and Chapter 10, Childproof: Protecting Your Child.)

Certificates of Deposit (CDs).   These are a type of savings account that pay a much higher rate than a passbook account if you agree to leave your funds in the bank for a specified length of time. The period may range from seven days to several years; the longer you commit the deposit, the higher your rate of interest. You can withdraw the earned interest, but you will be charged a penalty on early withdrawal of the principal. Rates vary from bank to bank, as do the methods of computing the rate.

THE TRUST DEPARTMENT

You're in good company if, like Vivian, you think the trust department of a bank functions primarily after a death by administering the estate. "The trust department doesn't do any good once somebody's dead," explains Teri Wilder, an officer of the Bank of America. "You need to preserve the assets in advance."

   As Vivian found out, trust departments can simplify your financial situation at any time. In addition to acting as trustees and/or administrators of estates, they offer two other services: custodial and investment management accounts.

Custodial account.   This type of account provides convenience, security, and freedom from the recordkeeping details of a financial portfolio. The trust department will collect dividends and interest, exercise options, and furnish a complete record of all transactions for your personal investment and tax information. It distributes income and principal, and makes investment changes, all as you direct. You retain title to the securities, and can amend or terminate the account at any time.

Investment management account.   This offers all the convenience of a custodial account, but includes investment advice. Remember that banks are generally conservative; they look to both preserve and enhance the client's estate, so they will balance safety against return.

The fees for trust department services are set by each individual bank, but generally they are all competitive. The fees you pay the trust department for financial advice, like those you pay to any financial advisor, are tax deductible.

TRUST DEPARTMENT OR FINANCIAL ADVISOR?

Why use the trust department of a bank and not an investment advisor or broker?

Many of the financial services overlap as banks provide investment services and investment houses offer banking services, but the trust departments of banks offer a wider range of services under one roof to people who are too busy or not sufficiently knowledgeable to take care of their investments.

Trust departments administer living trusts (see Chapter 8, Planning Your Estate). They manage real and commercial property, pay real estate taxes, and file for delinquent rent. They also sell certificates of deposit and municipal bonds. They have investment counselors, trust officers, and attorneys available for consultation, and they work closely with a client's lawyer and accountant. "We put everything together," says Kathleen Ethridge, trust officer with Santa Monica Bank. "We manage the whole."

To manage your account, trust departments usually require a minimum estate, often around $100,000, which may or may not exclude real estate assets. Many investment advisors have a similar, or higher, required minimum, although brokerage houses do not.

As with the advice given to those with investment management accounts, trust departments tend to be conservative "unless the client directs us otherwise," says Ms. Ethridge.

AN ENVIRONMENT OF CHANGE

Financial institutions are constantly developing new services and concepts to win your business. Take advantage of this competitive environment by regularly re-evaluating your needs and determining which financial institutions can best meet them.

BORROWING

5

At some point in their lives, many people need—or want—to borrow money or raise cash quickly. And that's when most of them discover they don't know how to do it. Three of the people we interviewed had the same urgent need and no idea what to do.

Kathy is a young teacher from Kansas whose husband, Dan, always paid the bills. Playing tennis one morning, Dan collapsed with a serious heart attack. After four weeks in intensive care, and four more weeks in the hospital, he was sent home and ordered to rest there for two more months— no pressure, no stress.

Dan is in his late thirties with an excellent job as a pension actuary. Since his future looked so secure, he and Kathy had stretched their budget the previous year and put all their savings into a down payment on a new home. Now Dan was confined to it, prevented from going back to work.

"It was a stressful period because Dan was chafing at the bit," said Kathy. "One day I opened the mail and, to my dismay, saw that a huge tax bill was due. At the time, Dan was the last person I could bother about it, and I had no idea how to come up with the money." Fortunately, Kathy discovered she could borrow from the cash build-up in Dan's life insurance policy.

Nan is a talented cook whose cakes and cookies had a mouth-watering reputation in her community. Through word of mouth, she was besieged with orders from friends and strangers. Sensing a business opportunity, she decided to open a small specialized bakery in a neighborhood shopping center.

When she went to the bank for a loan to buy commercial cooking equipment, she was surprised to find that the past success of Nan's Fancies and the list of standing orders didn't satisfy the loan officer. "The officer asked me what I was going to put up as collateral, and everything I suggested turned out to be in my husband's name," she said. "Except my jewelry, and he wouldn't accept that." Nan didn't get the loan until her husband co-signed it.

Margaret was recently divorced. Her husband took the sports car and left her the station wagon, but she decided she preferred the ease and low-cost mileage of a sporty compact. "I wanted to finance the car instead of paying cash, so I'd have some funds available in case an investment opportunity came along," she said.

On her first visit to the bank Margaret discovered she didn't have a credit rating, and was therefore not considered a good credit risk. "I couldn't believe it!" she said, outraged. "I always paid my bills on time—and I've been known to run up some pretty big bills." Unfortunately, Margaret never realized that since all the charge and credit cards were in her husband's name, he was the one with the credit rating, not she. She had to pay cash for the car.

Few people are financially savvy about raising money, let alone quickly. But borrowing is a skill you can learn. Preparation is the key. You have to be ready on two fronts: first, you must know what resources you have, and second, you have to know how you can use them. This chapter is a road map through that unfamiliar terrain.

The first step is to review your total assets. If you've completed worksheets 14 and 15, you're halfway home and the accountant and loan officer will bless you. If you haven't, now is the time. You'll need this information whether you go to a bank for a loan or convert any of your assets into cash.

BORROWING FROM FINANCIAL INSTITUTIONS

Three rules will ease your passage in the world of lending: First, speak only to a loan officer who has the authority to make the loan. Second, establish credit for yourself *before* you need it. You can do this by borrowing money from a bank *now*. Present a valid reason for the loan—this may include taxes, a reasonable vacation, or furniture, but don't tell the lender you are borrowing simply to establish credit for yourself. They usually won't lend on that basis. Third, be prepared to show you are a good credit risk so that the officer can justify your loan.

Basically, there are two different types of loans: those that require collateral and those that don't. A collateralized loan is secured by some type of asset, like the cash in a savings account, savings certificates, certificates of deposit, or stock in a publicly held company. With banks you can sometimes use other fixed assets, like a car or real property, as security, but usually not jewelry, furs, art, or silverware.

Secured, or Collateralized, Loans

To determine how much money to lend you on a secured loan and how to structure your repayment, the lending institution will evaluate the assets you put up as collateral. Some assets make better collateral than others.

Stocks and bonds. These are the easiest type of collateral because the bank knows it can convert them to cash if you default on your loan. Banks prefer securities listed on the American or New York Stock Exchange, but will consider over-the-counter stocks. They will normally loan between 60 percent and 70 percent of the current market price of a stock, and a higher amount on bonds (depending on the type of bond).

Cash. Strangely enough, cash is also a form of collateral. You can borrow against your cash, and still leave it in a certificate of deposit or a savings account. This has the dual benefit of leaving your savings undisturbed and establishing credit for yourself.

Real estate. Because the bank must determine a value and doesn't want to be in the real estate business of selling the property if you default, real estate is a complicated collateral. When you offer your home as security, the bank or savings and loan will appraise it to determine if your actual equity in the property covers the loan you are seeking. Moreover, bank appraisers normally assess your property conservatively.

Real estate loans can also be expensive. To get the loan you usually pay "points," which can vary from 1.5 percent to 4 percent or more of the amount of the loan, depending on the prevailing economic climate. You might also have to pay for the bank's title policy. Real estate loans are time-consuming and often take six weeks to process, so they are not a good source of emergency cash.

Automobiles. These are accepted as security for some kinds of loans by some financial institutions. Normally, you can borrow up to 70 percent of the *Kelly Blue Book* value.

Jewelry, furs, art, and silver. Although not acceptable security at most banks, these will be considered by finance companies.

Co-signing. This is a form of collateral. The bank will recognize the value of a co-signer's assets in granting you a loan. Be sure the co-signer recognizes his obligation if you default on the loan. Even though Nan's husband, as co-signer, was prepared to repay her loan, she repaid it herself out of her business profits (which also helped her establish her credit with the bank).

Keep careful track of all guarantees in the *Collateral Guarantee or Co-Signature Record* (#20) worksheet at the end of the book. You never know when you'll need this information.

Unsecured, or Uncollateralized, Loans

Obviously, the stronger your credit position with a bank, the less likely you are to need collateral for a loan. (See Chapter 6, Establishing Credit, for how and why to establish a credit rating.)

If you're seeking an unsecured loan, you must justify your ability to repay it. Be prepared to reassure the lender with strong answers to these questions:

Do you have a steady income?

How long have you worked at that job?

Do you have a credit history?

Did you repay previous loans satisfactorily?

What is your repayment record with department stores and credit cards?

Note: A common misconception is that you must have a job to qualify for a loan. A woman can get a loan based on her husband's income, although he may have to co-sign the loan agreement. This loan can be either secured or unsecured, depending on his financial record.

Personal Guarantees

Anytime you apply for a business or a substantial personal loan, you will probably be asked to act as a guarantor on that loan. That means you'll be held personally responsible for any default on the loans if the original collateral is inadequate, and the lender can legally sue you for repayment. This differs from regular collateral because you are putting any and all of your assets at risk up to the amount of the loan, rather than pledging a specific item, like a stock or a bond.

This provision may seem harmless, but it could haunt you if you don't repay the loan because your personal assets—not just your business or corporate assets—are now vulnerable. Avoid signing a personal guarantee on loans if at all possible. Many times you have no choice; it may be the only way you can get a loan.

If you must sign a guarantee to obtain a loan, be sure to keep a record of exactly what you have guaranteed, and whom it is for. (This is important information for your heirs.) People often forget they have guaranteed a loan for someone else, only to end up making the payments themselves because the borrower failed to make them. Use the *Collateral Guarantee or Co-Signature Record* (#20) worksheet to keep track of these obligations.

Shopping for a Loan

Some interest rates for loans can be deceptive. Be sure to review the "Truth in Lending Statement" before you sign the loan agreement. This statement, which is federally required of the lender, clearly spells out the full details of the loan. When shopping for a loan, use the *Loan Interest Rate Comparison* (#21) worksheet to evaluate rates offered by competing lenders.

OTHER SOURCES FOR READY CASH

Bank loans are not the only way to raise cash. In fact, they sometimes take so long to process that you must turn to other sources if your needs are urgent.

The first step is to identify all your sources of ready cash. We describe the most common assets below, and divide them into immediate sources for cash and secondary sources where you can raise funds. Use the *Emergency Cash Plan* (#22) worksheet to lay out all your options.

Note: Get a power of attorney from your spouse (and anyone else who holds title to these assets) so you can convert them to cash in an emergency.

Immediate Sources for Cash

Checking account reserve. Decide on a minimum balance and keep that reserve constantly available in your account.

Overdraft account. If you don't already have an overdraft account with your bank, make arrangements for one. This account (it goes by different names in different banks, for example, "Redi Reserve," "Instant Cash," "Overdraft Protection," or "Automatic Loan Advance") gives you a prearranged line of credit on your checking account that allows you to write checks larger than your bank balance. You can get overdraft protection up to $5,000, depending on your financial strength and your relationship with the bank. You don't pay extra for this type of account if you don't use that feature.

Savings account. An obvious source of quick cash is whatever emergency reserve you decide to maintain in your savings account. Remember that certain financial institutions, particularly certain savings and loans, have time limitations on withdrawals. Be sure you understand those limitations so that these funds are truly available to you if needed.

Money market funds. A money market fund with a bank or a "non-bank" is an excellent source of liquid cash, and normally yields a higher rate of interest than a savings account.

Cashable securities. Stocks and bonds are another source for cash. If you don't want to sell your securities when you need cash, you can borrow 60 percent to 70 percent of their current value from a bank.

Credit card limits. Each of your credit cards has an approved credit limit available to you. It usually appears on your monthly statements. Ask each credit card company how to qualify for a higher limit, even though you have no immediate need for it. This is an additional source of quick funds, although the interest rates are high. (See Chapter 6, Establishing Credit, for ways to get individual credit cards.)

Undisbursed loan.   Some banks will grant you and your spouse a joint personal line of credit by establishing what is called an undisbursed loan; the bank agrees to the amount in advance, activates the loan immediately on request, and charges interest only when it disburses the funds. You'll probably pay the prevailing rate of interest at the time you need the money, but you have the security of knowing a sizable sum of cash is available in an emergency. You don't have to take the total loan at one time; you use whatever amounts you need incrementally.

Joint revolving line of credit.   If your bank won't give you an undisbursed loan, ask about a joint revolving line of credit. Like an undisbursed loan, you and the bank agree on the amount of future credit, but the bank reviews the arrangement periodically, usually every three to six months.
   This type of credit has several desirable features:

- The interest can be based on a commercial rate, which is considerably lower than the rate for cash advanced in an overdraft account.
- You don't have to use the entire loan limit, but only the amount you need.

Secondary Sources for Cash

Secondary sources are not a lesser way of raising cash; they just usually take longer to get the funds.

Life insurance policies.   You can borrow on some life insurance policies, and the rate of interest is often attractively low. Ask your insurance agent for the cash value, if any, of your life insurance policies and those you have on your children. The type of life insurance you own determines whether or not this is a source of ready cash for you; if you have term life insurance, there probably isn't any cash value. (For a detailed explanation of life insurance and its cash value, see Chapter 11, The Role of Life Insurance.)
   Ask your life insurance agent to send you the loan papers in advance so you can incorporate them in your emergency cash plan and, if needed, activate this source without delay.

Credit union.   Find out how you can borrow from your credit union. Complete all necessary forms in advance and put them in your file for the future.

Profit-sharing plan.   Check the terms for borrowing from your profit-sharing plan in an emergency. If certain forms are required, complete them in advance and file them for future use.

Personal loan companies. There are many reputable personal loan companies whose primary business is making short-term loans. Don't ignore them as a source of secondary cash, even if you already have a bank loan.

Car loan. If you have a car loan, ask the lender about refinancing your present loan. If he refuses, ask another lender to refinance the loan. You should be able to borrow 80 percent of the *Kelly Blue Book* value of the car. If you don't currently have a car loan, this is the time to get one.

Sell car. A car is an excellent source of immediate cash. Your bank or a neighborhood automobile dealer can determine its value in the *Kelly Blue Book*. Remember to deduct any loans you have against it.

Take a second or third mortgage on your home. If you already have a second mortgage, consider refinancing it with the present lender, or another lender, to get additional cash. Mortgage rates will vary with the current lending climate.

Change your state and federal income tax withholding amounts. You can reduce the amount of tax withheld from your paycheck and increase your net cash spendable income by changing your withholding amounts. If you're self-employed, work with your accountant in changing your tax estimates. Be certain you stay within I.R.S. rules to avoid any year-end tax penalties.

Pawn jewelry. This is a drastic step for a dire emergency. Before you take it, make sure you understand how to redeem the jewelry under your state's laws. With a pawn shop you can either borrow against the article you are pawning or actually sell the item to the shop. If you borrow, you have a designated time period to retrieve the item. During that period, you pay interest far in excess of bank rates but normally governed by the laws in that state.

Friends or relatives. If you're in a real bind, don't hesitate to approach friends or relatives for a temporary loan, but be businesslike. Formalize your arrangement with a promissory note that clearly states the terms of the loan, and how and when you will repay it. If you pay them a fair interest rate, you may feel less reluctant to seek their aid and they may accept interest-only payments for a specified period to help keep your initial obligation low.

Employer. If you have worked for the same employer for a long time and have a good relationship, consider asking him to act as a guarantor on a bank loan or to give you a personal loan through his business. Your selling points: the boss knows you can repay the loan through your employment (periodic loan deductions from your paycheck can be arranged), and relieving your mental stress will benefit your work.

Keogh or IRA accounts. Keogh funds have no loan provisions, but there are provisions for "hardship" withdrawals. You will pay a 10 percent penalty for premature withdrawal and you'll be taxed on the withdrawn amount.

You may "borrow" from your IRA account for up to sixty days without penalty, as long as you document both the withdrawal and deposit. If you "borrow" from your account beyond sixty days, you must pay a 10 percent penalty on the entire amount in the account.

As you can see, when you need to borrow money, the better prepared you are, the less you'll have to pay for it. Before you go for a loan, look over the worksheets for the chapters Figuring Your Net Worth, Banking, Establishing Credit, and Budgeting. You'll find them helpful.

ESTABLISHING CREDIT

Credit is like a passport. You never think of getting it until you need it—and then you're stuck until it comes through. Or, worse yet, you had it and you let it lapse.

That's what happened to Marlene, who in her single days had been an airline stewardess. "I had a good job, and it wasn't a problem to get credit cards and gas charge cards. But I made the mistake of letting them lapse after I got married."

Now, like a great many people, Marlene doesn't have a credit rating. If you're in the same boat, it's probably for one of the following reasons:

- You've never worked, so you couldn't establish credit.
- You worked but you didn't bother to establish credit when you had the chance.
- You're a woman and you had credit but you lost it after you got married and failed to notify credit bureaus of your new name.
- You're a nonworking wife who doesn't have assets in your own name to support a credit rating.

It's not too late for you to rectify this situation. In fact, it's vitally important that you establish credit as soon as possible.

As our friend Margaret, eyeing a sporty compact, says (practically every day), "If I only had a credit rating, I'd have my new car and could unload this gas-guzzling monster!"

CREDIT AND WHERE TO GET IT

Credit is the ability to borrow money or to buy goods without cash. With credit, you can purchase goods and services from future income and you don't need to carry large amounts of cash.

In order to get credit, you need a good credit rating. You have to show that you're a good risk, that you can pay for the goods you've purchased and/or repay the funds you've borrowed, promptly and in full. It's harder to convince lenders that you're credit-worthy when you don't have an independent job or assets of your own, but it can be done.

The best time to secure credit is when you don't need it, because that's when it's easiest to get. It takes time and you should do it carefully. Here are the proper steps to take in order to establish your own credit rating.

Open Your Own Bank Account

Begin to establish your financial identity by opening checking and savings accounts in your name alone, not a joint account. And make sure it's your legal name—for women a legal name may be Mary Jones, Mary B. Jones, or Mrs. Mary Jones, but it is not Mrs. John Jones; for men it is John Jones, not "Bud" Jones. To get your own credit you need at least a checking account. Your bank accounts will not appear on your credit history, but they set the stage for future borrowing.

Pay the Household Bills

Put the utilities and telephone in your legal name, or at least in joint names with your spouse, and pay those bills out of *your* checking account. This will help you establish credit, and it will avoid problems if your spouse dies.

Take Out a Loan

If possible, take out a small loan with your local bank or credit union, even if you don't need the money. By repaying the loan promptly, you'll establish a good track record that will be invaluable for future credit references. Co-signing on your spouse's loans won't help your credit rating. Make sure the loan is in force for one year so that it appears on your credit rating. Banks call this a "rated" loan. (Chapter 5 has more information on loans.)

Credit Cards and Charge Cards

Get credit cards and charge cards in your own name only, even if you and your spouse already have joint cards. They are an inexpensive way of building your credit history because they carry no charges if you pay within a certain length of time. Moreover, cards held in joint names do not help you establish your own credit, and they may be canceled at your spouse's death, at which time you might have difficulty securing new ones in your own name.

If you can't get a card in your own name, have your spouse initially co-sign for you. This will still establish your credit. After one year, request your own card, since by then you will have established a credit-worthy payment record.

Pay all bills on all your cards promptly. The next year, request higher limits on your credit cards, even though you may not need it at the time.

Get both credit and charge cards. They are not the same, but both are excellent ways of establishing your credit rating.

Credit cards (MasterCard or Visa, for example).   These are primarily issued through a bank—unlike charge or convenience cards—and carry an annual fee and interest rates. Fees, interest rates, and finance charges vary from card to card and from bank to bank. Sometimes the same bank charges different fees and interest rates depending on the state in which you live.

All credit cards can charge varying interest rates, usually ranging between 12 percent and 24 percent per year, depending on the laws of the state in which they operate. With most credit cards, there is no interest charge if you pay within a specified time (about twenty-five days).

If the interest charges in your state are high, you can apply for a card from the same bank in another state. Write the American Financial Services Association, 1101 Fourteenth Street, N.W., Washington, D.C. 20005, for its Summary of Consumer Credit Laws and Rates.

Charge cards.   These are normally department store and gasoline cards. Unlike credit cards, with which you can secure cash, charge cards only entitle you to purchase goods and services from the company that issued the card.

Convenience or credit cards (American Express and Diner's Club, for example).   These cards charge fees that are higher than credit card fees, but bill interest or finance charges only if you pay late. Unlike charge cards, with these you are expected to pay the entire balance when it is due. Although these convenience cards allow you a few days grace, they will cancel your credit if you consistently pay late. A canceled card would be disastrous to your credit rating, so protect that rating by always paying on time.

Once you have received credit, request a review of your credit file annually from each credit source to make sure it's accurate.

YOUR CREDIT APPLICATION

An understanding of how credit is approved will help you improve your chances for a good rating. To see if you're a good credit risk, study the list of Credit Danger Signals on page 46. If your score is too high, change some of your spending habits before applying for credit.

Most credit decisions are made on the basis of the following questions:

Stability.   How long have you lived in the area? How long at your present address? Do you own or rent? Do you have a telephone, savings account, or investments?

Income.   What is your occupation? Is it year-round or seasonal? How long have you worked for this employer, and are you paid by salary or commissions? (You must have either income or assets to qualify for credit.)

Debt record.   How much money do you currently owe? How do you pay your bills? How often do you borrow, and for what reasons? (A declared bankruptcy or property repossession will be a major handicap.)

Expenses.   How many dependents do you have? What is your life-style?

In considering these general questions, most credit or reporting agencies use their own system of scoring to evaluate your credit application.

If You Have Credit Problems

If you're notified you don't qualify for credit, or that credit is denied for any reason, take these steps:

First, call the person who signed the letter to make sure that no mistake was made.

Second, request in writing the reason for the denial. Look at the two sample letters, Request for Credit Information and Request for Credit Profile (pages 47 and 48), and use either to request the information.

Third, if you receive a poor credit listing, first find out the name of the reporting agency from the people from whom you are seeking credit—by law they must tell you. Then ask the reporting agency for a copy of your negative credit report—use the Request for Credit Profile sample letter. When you receive your credit file from the reporting agency, review it against the actions suggested in the Checklist for Your Credit File (page 49).

Finally, if you have already established good credit with a department store, bank, or elsewhere, ask them for the names of their credit agencies. Contact those agencies—most will be listed in the Yellow Pages under "Credit Reporting Agencies"—for their favorable credit report on you, and forward it to the company that has denied you credit.

Your Credit Rights

Under the Equal Credit Opportunity Act, no one can discriminate on the basis of race, color, religion, national origin, sex, marital status, or age. If you think this has occurred, you can make a formal complaint under the Act. If you need assistance, contact the Consumer Credit Counselor Organization in your area. This is a nonprofit organization supported by contributions from the business community, and it specializes in credit and debt counseling. You can also contact the National Foundation for Consumer Credit, Inc., 1819 H Street, Washington, D.C. 20006.

In addition, make use of the federal Fair Credit Reporting Act, which is helpful in keeping your credit records current and complete. Among the many rights you have under this Act, you can review your credit file at any organization at any time, know who received your credit report, correct information in your credit report, remove adverse information after seven years, and sue a reporting agency for damages.

As you can see, a number of government agencies will help you protect your rights. You don't have to face any of these problems alone, and in most cases, you don't have to hire legal counsel to do it for you.

CREDIT
DANGER
SIGNALS

		Yes	No
1.	Do you spend more than 40 percent of your monthly income on rent, condo, or mortgage payments?	[✓]	[ ]
2.	Do your credit payments exceed 25 percent of your take-home pay?	[ ]	[✓]
3.	Do you delay one bill so you can pay another?	[ ]	[✓]
4.	Are you receiving past due notices on any bills?	[ ]	[✓]
5.	Are you charging more each month than the payments you make on your credit accounts?	[ ]	[✓]
6.	Do you run out of money before pay day?	[ ]	[✓]
7.	Do you take increasingly more time to pay off balances on your accounts?	[✓]	[ ]
8.	Are you using credit card advances to cover everyday living expenses?	[ ]	[✓]
9.	Are you unable to save a little money each month?	[ ]	[✓]
10.	Do you use your charge accounts when you know you may not be able to meet the payments?	[ ]	[✓]
11.	Do you use credit cards to go on buying sprees?	[ ]	[✓]
12.	Do you depend on extra income such as overtime to get you through each month?	[ ]	[✓]
13.	Have you requested loan extensions from your creditors?	[ ]	[✓]
14.	Are you paying no more than the minimum on your charge cards or other bills?	[ ]	[✓]
15.	Have you ever made unrealistic promises to your creditors?	[ ]	[✓]
16.	Do you fear that your employer will learn the extent of your total debts?	[ ]	[✓]
17.	Does the size of your debts bother you?	[✓]	[ ]

If you have more than 5 yes answers, you have a major credit and spending problem.

FROM: _____   DATE: _____ 19____

_____

_____

Dear Credit Manager:

Please report all information concerning the account below in both of our names, as provided for by the Equal Credit Opportunity Act, Regulation B.

NAME: _____

          First   *Middle*   *Last*

SPOUSE'S NAME: _____

                  First   *Middle*   *Last*

_____

NAME IN WHICH ACCOUNT IS LISTED (*name on the billing statement*)

_____

ACCOUNT NUMBER

                          _____

                                    Signature

SAMPLE LETTER: REQUEST FOR CREDIT PROFILE

FROM: _____   DATE: _____ 19____

_____   FILE NO. _____

_____

Dear Sir or Madam:

Please send me a copy of my credit profile. The following is the pertinent information:

NAME: _____
           First   *Middle*   *Last*

SOC. SEC. #: _____

BIRTHDATE: _____
           Month   *Date*   *Year*

PRESENT RESIDENCE: _____

_____

_____

PAST RESIDENCES IN LAST FIVE YEARS:

1. _____

_____

_____

2. _____

_____

_____

_____
Signature

Check One:

[ ]   Check enclosed.

[ ]   I have been denied credit within the past thirty days as a result of information from your credit file.

[ ]   There is an error in the information in my credit file.

1. Learn the nature and substance of all the information in your file.

2. Find out the name of each of the businesses (or other sources) that supplied information on you to the reporting agency.

3. Learn the names of everyone who received reports on you within the past six months (or the last two years if the reports were for employment purposes).

4. Request the reporting agency to reinvestigate and correct or delete information that was found to be inaccurate, incomplete, or obsolete.

5. Follow up to determine the results of the reinvestigation.

6. Ask the reporting agency, at no cost to you, to notify those you name who received reports within the past six months (two years if for employment purposes) that certain information was deleted.

7. Demand that your version of the facts be placed in your file if the reinvestigation did not settle the dispute.

8. If you are willing to pay a reasonable fee, request the reporting agency to send your statement of the dispute to those you name who received reports containing the disputed information within the past six months (two years if received for employment purposes).

BUDGETING

"There are people who have absolutely no idea how much money they are spending or what it costs them to live, and for a long time I was one of them," said Bruce, a suburban Detroit man who works in a bookstore. For over a year, while his wife was sick, and then hospitalized, he struggled to manage the household accounts and write the monthly checks.

Bruce's checkbook woes may sound depressingly familiar to you. "I didn't exactly manage the expenses," he explained. "It was more like muddling through. I'd get a big bill, like the semi-annual life insurance premium, and I'd put it aside, hoping to accumulate enough extra money from my salary and some dividends in time to cover it."

"Muddling through" money matters isn't acceptable to everyone, especially if you're trying to learn to handle your own affairs, as Patti was. Patti, the wife of a successful lawyer, realized about three years ago that she didn't know much about money management.

"All of a sudden I got nervous. I didn't know how to take care of myself or what it cost to run a house. When I told my husband my fears, he became very angry." Patti recalled his outburst. "He said, 'Don't expect me to teach you in a short time what it took me years to learn! Go and study yourself.' I guess I really touched a nerve by suggesting I wanted to be able to take care of myself," said Patti, shrugging her shoulders.

Eventually, Patti's husband agreed to set up a budget. Each was to keep track of and write checks for half the expenses. Patti recited the list of what she pays: the rent, the utilities, insurance, automobile repairs, her clothing, the kids' clothing, groceries, dry cleaning—all those kinds of expenses. "I write a hundred checks a month, and I balance the checkbook and keep track of how much is left in each category for the next month," she said. "And that's only half the checks!"

What bothers Patti is how little she still understands about budgeting, even though she puts in so much time at it. Paul pays for everything else, like travel. "A trip is a big lump sum of cash. How does he know there's enough money for that trip? I haven't learned to do that. I really still have no idea how much money we spend each month or what we can afford."

As most of us find out the hard way, one of the important steps in a financial education is gaining control of our own finances. We all have to learn how to manage those mandatory expenses we must pay for. A harder lesson is knowing what we can afford to do with our discretionary funds. In spite of Patti's bewilderment, budgeting is the best way you can learn. Budgeting helps you locate money you didn't know you had and direct it where you want it, as we show you in this chapter.

We know people despair at the thought of making—and sticking to—a budget, but you'll also discover there's an up side to what we agree is a tedious task. For one, a budget acts as a brake whenever you're tempted to overcharge on a credit card. For another, a budget will help you get a loan because it demonstrates to lending institutions that you have control of your finances. And best of all, for your diligence and discipline in budget-keeping, you may be rewarded by finding extra funds that you can spend any way you want—a budget bonus.

Budgeting Worksheets

The budgeting worksheets (#s 23–27) in the Workbook section will help you identify where you spend your money. As soon as you record your actual expenses, you'll see which ones are mandatory and which are discretionary. Then you'll be able to make thoughtful decisions about expenses you can eliminate and those you must pay.

The *Daily Cash Budgeting Worksheet* (#23) tracks your money on a day-to-day basis, so you can see where all your cash is going. List everything you spend each day; at the end of a week, evaluate your daily expenses and decide if you want to institute some controls over the cash. This will remind you to evaluate each such expenditure carefully in terms of your overall budget.

The *Monthly Expense Budgeting Worksheet* (#24) is for those of you who are really serious about budgeting and want to measure your expenses for one entire month before completing a working budget.

The *Annual Expense Budgeting Worksheet* (#25) tallies all your expenses for the year, and enables you to translate each item into an average monthly amount. Some of your expenses only occur once a year, some are seasonal, others are monthly. To estimate the monthly cost of items you pay annually, divide the total by twelve and enter that monthly average. If you have seasonal costs—such as swimming pool maintenance—or quarterly bills—such as tax returns for household employees—divide the annual totals by twelve to get monthly averages.

After you have completed the *Annual Expense Budgeting Worksheet* (#25) you'll have an average monthly amount for every item. Total those monthly amounts to see how your total monthly expenses compare with your total monthly income. If your income exceeds your expenses, consider where you want to commit more funds. If your expenses are larger than your income, review the worksheet to see where you can reduce or eliminate discretionary purchases.

The mathematics are simple: If you need, or want, more discretionary income, you must either increase your income or reduce your expenses. Cutting expenses is easier. By listing all your noncritical outlays on the *Discretionary Expense Worksheet* (#26) you'll be able to see how much you can pick up in each category and where you want to control your spending.

A *Monthly Budget Control Worksheet* (#27) will help you focus on your balance of payments. When you've decided how you want to balance your own budget, enter on the *Monthly Budget Control Worksheet* (#27) the monthly total of all discretionary purchases you plan to eliminate. By reconciling your intended monthly savings with your available monthly income, you'll get your monthly expense budget.

Once you've prepared a budget, start to pay the family bills yourself. Pay all of them, not just some of them. That's the only way you'll get a total picture of your family's expenses. To keep you on track, at least every three months measure your actual expenditures against your budget, and make budgetary corrections as needed.

PROTECTING
YOUR
ASSETS

PLANNING YOUR ESTATE

The car accident that killed our friend John and badly injured Betty taught us a good deal about getting our family affairs in order. As we tried to help Betty, it became evident that a lot of the financial problems she encountered could have been prevented by proper preplanning.

For instance, Betty badly needed some cash after several months in the hospital. "I tried to sell some blue chip stocks we were holding for an emergency," she said. "But my stockbroker told me that since they were registered in John's name, I couldn't sell them until they passed through probate. He said if we'd only owned the stocks as joint tenants, they would have come to me automatically."

Betty shook her head, finding it hard to believe that such a small change could make such a big difference. "When John bought the stock years ago, he never even thought about title of ownership."

How you own securities is just one item that can make a critical difference in a financial crunch. How do you own everything else? Who holds title to your home? Your car? In whose name are the bank accounts and money market funds listed? If you are part owner of a business, what happens if you want to sell your share, or if you die?

To our surprise, often the smartest businesspeople are careless about the legal structures of their businesses, as we found out from all too many widows. Barbara was one of them.

Barbara was a young woman whose pleasant face always seemed clouded. And no wonder, when we heard her story.

Her husband, Jim, started a software consulting business. When it grew too big for him to manage alone, he took in a partner. They wrote a partnership agreement, but it didn't spell out what would happen if either of them died. They were both young, and the future seemed infinite.

Then Jim died suddenly of a heart attack. The loyalty Jim's partner had for him ended at Jim's death. Without a buy-and-sell agreement, Barbara found herself in an adversarial position with a once-friendly business partner who turned hostile and combative. The wrangle over the value of the company and Barbara's share was long and acrimonious, and it cost Barbara more than she could afford. After a year with no resolution, she lost her house and had to move to a small apartment with her two young children.

"If Jim had worked out a buy-and-sell agreement with his partner—in writing—my life would be drastically different from what it is right now," she said bitterly.

Sadly, what happened to Barbara and Betty is quite common. But it doesn't have to happen to you.

No matter how big or little it is, everyone has an estate. It consists of all your possessions—not just everything you own, but also everything you owe. You're selling your family short if you don't try to protect it.

In this chapter and the next, you'll get a brief overview of how to safeguard your estate, and how to plan for its distribution. We will deal with probate—a court procedure that changes the legal ownership of your property after you die and makes sure your will is valid and your assets are properly distributed. It's an expensive, inconvenient, and lengthy process you may want to avoid. You'll also find valuable suggestions for the financial security of your children. You may not be an estate planner after you read these two chapters, but the *List of Ownership of Assets* (#28) and the *Estate Planning Checklist* (#29) will provide you with sound questions and organized information that will enable your advisors to do their best for you.

THE MANY WAYS OF OWNERSHIP

As Betty discovered, how you own your property may determine how your assets will pass, and to whom, on the death of the owner.

You can own (hold title) to property in various ways, each of which has benefits and/or consequences for you.

Separate property. This is property owned solely by one person. You can sell it, give it away, or will it to anyone at any time without the consent or permission of anyone else.

Joint tenancy. This involves ownership by two or more individuals. If you're a joint tenant, you have an equal, undivided share with the other joint tenants during your lifetime. As a joint tenant, you may sell or give away your share, but you may not will it away. If a joint tenant dies, that share automatically passes to the other joint tenants without having to pass through probate.

Tenancy in common. This also involves two or more owners, but each owner doesn't necessarily have an equal share. As a tenant in common, you may sell, give, or will your share of the property without the consent of the other tenants in common.

Community property.   A form of ownership that exists in eight states, this is property acquired during marriage. During your lifetime, neither you nor your spouse may sell or give away any of the community property without the other's consent. But on death, either of you can will away your half of the community property; the other half belongs to the survivor.

All gifts or inheritances you receive are separate from your community property, and if you want to keep them separate, be sure they don't get mixed up with community property, or they'll be presumed to be community.

There are tax advantages to community property ownership. When either you or your spouse dies, the tax basis for both halves of the community property is raised to current market value, reducing the capital gains tax.

On the *List of Ownership of Assets* (#28) worksheet, located in the Workbook section, record the way in which all your family property is owned. It will help your lawyer and accountant coordinate your tax and estate planning needs.

BUY-AND-SELL AGREEMENTS

Even though participation in a business is often the biggest asset a person has, inexplicably all too many businesspeople don't have buy-and-sell agreements with their partners or their company. This agreement should spell out precisely what happens when participants want to sell their shares, or if they die or are disabled. The absence of such an agreement is a profound oversight that leaves the survivors vulnerable to financial difficulties. Don't let that happen to you.

Even if you don't have a problem with your spouse's partner, you will certainly have to confront a different adversary—the Internal Revenue Service. Without a valid buy-and-sell agreement, the I.R.S. will set a value on the business to determine the estate tax. You and your partners should establish the value of the business, rather than leave the survivors to negotiate with the I.R.S.

Be certain to initiate or update a buy-and-sell agreement—and make sure it applies to disability as well as death. This agreement is just as important to all the partners, because any agreement that protects you will protect their heirs as well. It's the most professional and easiest way for all of you to receive an equitable share of the business.

Note: You can use life insurance to create a fund to cover a buy-and-sell agreement. The cash from the life insurance policy would immediately buy the other shares of the business.

TRUSTS

"Thank God Bill set up that fund for the college tuition!" said Nan, the cook who started Nan's Fancies. "We never would have been able to pay for three kids at school—not at today's rates—if he hadn't planned for it when they were still in grade school."

What Nan was blessing was a particular trust, one of many that can solve a variety of your financial situations—if you know about them in time.

There are different kinds of trusts, each with advantages and disadvantages, and each meeting particular needs. You can set them up to take care of elderly parents, to control spendthrift children, or to subsidize your firstborn, who wants to write the Great American Novel. You decide how long they'll run, and who administers them. But for all their differences, trusts share certain characteristics.

Technically, a trust is a legal agreement between two parties—the grantor and the trustee—to hold, administer, and distribute your property for the benefit of your heirs. You, the grantor, name as trustee a family member, a financially astute friend, or a professional trustee, such as an attorney, an accountant, a bank, or a trust company. All trustees receive legal title to the property placed in the trust, and must follow the instructions you give in the trust agreement. Professional trustees charge an annual fee based on the size of the trust.

Trusts are complicated. You need an attorney who specializes in estate planning to advise you on the type that best fits your financial situation and objectives. But you'll help your advisors if you understand some common trusts and what they can do.

Testamentary trust. These trusts are usually established to manage property for heirs who lack financial knowledge and experience. Suppose you want to name your sister as guardian for your children because she's the one who will take care of their day-to-day needs best, but she isn't capable of making investment decisions. For their financial care you establish a testamentary trust with an experienced money manager. You create this trust by designating it in your will, which means your estate must be probated before the assets can be placed into the trust by a court order.

Living trust. The great merit of a living trust is that property placed in it doesn't pass through probate. It enables you to provide your family with funds for immediate expenses, plus an income upon your death. It protects the confidentiality of how you dispose of your property, and it minimizes court supervision over your property.

As the name implies, a living trust takes effect during your lifetime. Some you can end at any time, others you can limit to a certain number of years, or terminate at some event, for example when your children reach a certain age.

Generally, if you have a living trust, you also have a will that covers any assets not included in the trust. Your will and those remaining assets must go through probate.

A living trust must be either revocable or irrevocable. With a "revocable trust" you keep complete control of the property you put in the trust, and you can even act as your own trustee. You have the right to change the terms of the trust or end it anytime during your lifetime. Because you haven't relinquished control, the assets in the trust will be subject to estate and inheritance taxes.

In an "irrevocable trust," you give up control of the trust's assets and you can't alter its provisions for the life of the trust, which can run permanently or for a specific period of time. A major advantage of some irrevocable trusts is that assets are permanently removed from your estate, and therefore, aren't subject to taxes on your death.

While recent federal tax law changes allow you to leave your estate, no matter how large, to your spouse tax-free, only a limited amount can pass to your other heirs without being taxed. An irrevocable trust allows you to shelter appreciating property that you want to distribute to your heirs and don't need during your lifetime.

Although the tax benefits of removing assets from your estate are appealing, the loss of control with an irrevocable trust makes most of us feel uneasy.

Q-TIP (Qualified Terminal Interest Property) trust. This type of trust shelters its assets from estate taxes on a death, but is subject to estate taxes on the death of the surviving spouse. Its real benefit is that it allows you to provide for your spouse and still direct where your property goes after the death of the surviving spouse.

Charitable remainder trust. If you own appreciated property that is producing little or no income, you might use it to create this type of trust. It allows you to give away an asset, receive an income tax deduction, yet continue to collect earnings from the asset until the trust ends—that would be anytime from twenty years to the death of your beneficiary or yourself. The I.R.S. will calculate your charitable tax deduction based on your age, the size of your gift, and your rate of return; higher rates of return receive lower deductions.

As you can see, establishing a sound estate plan calls for professional advice. Work with your accountant, an estate planning specialist, and your attorney—and to maximize their talents and minimize your costs, be properly prepared for your meetings with them. The *Estate Planning Checklist* (#29) is a handy review and a good way to get ready. You'll be glad to see that most of the information you need for it comes from other worksheets in *A Family Survival Kit.*

DISTRIBUTING YOUR ASSETS

9

If there's one act most of us postpone, it's making a will. Not only do we want to avoid an unpleasant subject, but we fear we're somehow tempting fate. As our neighbor Tom put it, "When I sign my will, I hear a loud thunderclap in my head and the gods say, 'Okay, now that everything's in order, let's zap him!' Let me tell you, when I leave my lawyer's office, I'm very careful as I cross the street!"

The only reason Tom finally updated his will is because he loves to travel. In an informal survey we once made among our friends, every one confessed they usually reviewed their wills just before taking off on vacation. As one of them said, "Listen, we worry enough about the children when we're away from home. At least this is one way we feel we're protecting them if the plane crashes."

In our heads, of course, we know that's nonsense. Not having a will can be dangerous to your wealth. The most disastrous consequences are excessive inheritance and estate taxes, and prolonged probate (we'll explain that later in this chapter)—not to mention the mental anguish that accompanies them. When you hear Julie's all too typical story, you may want to call your lawyer right away.

Julie is the widow of a successful Los Angeles accountant, and it was hard to believe she was the unintended victim of poor estate planning. As Rob's will dragged through probate court, Julie realized that, like the proverbial shoemaker whose children went barefoot, Rob was always too busy at the office to put his own financial house in order.

"For five years after Rob died I had no idea of my financial situation," said Julie. "I was living in limbo until the estate was settled."

Inadvertently, Rob bequeathed Julie two common and widespread problems: the agony of a long, drawn-out probate to settle the estate and excessive taxes that significantly eroded his assets. Careful planning could have reduced both the delays and the financial losses in distributing his assets.

How can you avoid Julie's painful predicament? A proper will, conscientious executors, astute trustees, and an understanding of the probate procedure will help you distribute your estate the way you want to, efficiently and prudently. It's worth your while—and your assets—to understand the process.

WILLS

Your will is a tool for distributing your estate the way you want it distributed. It is simply a written document that conforms to the laws of your state and explains exactly where you want your assets to go after your death.

Aside from this, a will can serve to reduce your estate and inheritance taxes and eliminate the extra fees and costs incurred when you die without one. The law gives you many choices if you make a will, but none if you don't. With a will there's a way—your way.

When you're considering how to distribute your assets, use the *Will Preparation Worksheet* (#30) at the end of the book. It will help you keep track of your beneficiaries and your bequests to each of them.

Types of Wills

Formal will. This type of will should be prepared by an attorney. He'll know what important provisions to incorporate and will discuss them with you. Your will must be properly witnessed by at least two disinterested people, who should sign it in your presence.

Statutory will. This is a preprinted form with standard wording approved by your state's legislative body. Normally, these provisions are rigid and any changes from the standard wording risk violating the state law on wills and invalidating the document. If you choose a statutory will, make certain that you use the most current form, and that you recognize its limitations. You'll also need two valid witnesses to sign the will in your presence.

Holographic will. This is a handwritten document prepared by an individual. If you make one, write it entirely in your own handwriting. You don't need to have it witnessed, but you must date and sign it. The margin for error and ambiguity is so great that we strongly recommend against this type of will. Moreover, not all states accept holographic wills.

Intestate is the term used when you die without a valid will. In that case, your assets are distributed according to the intestate laws of your state of residence, except for real property, which is distributed under the state laws where it is located.

A court-appointed administrator will manage and distribute your assets, and his decisions may be quite different from what you would prefer. Your estate pays the administrator a fee, normally 3 percent to 5 percent of the value of the estate, and the cost of the mandatory bond he must post.

Note: A *living will* is a document specifying under what conditions you wish life-support systems to be discontinued. It is not a legally binding will for estate purposes, and is not recognized in all states.

As your personal or financial status changes, you might want to modify your will to be sure it always reflects your estate planning goals. Review your will every year; whenever there is a birth, death, marriage, or divorce in your family; when you change jobs or retire; have significant financial gains or losses; move to another state; or the state of your health changes. You'll find a detailed listing in the *When to Review a Will* (#31) worksheet.

You can always revise your will, but never make changes on the face of the original. Any additions, deletions, or erasures on the document after it is signed and witnessed can invalidate the will and, at the least, may delay the settlement of your estate.

Your attorney can amend the will with codicils that explain, add, or delete provisions in your existing will. If you make numerous changes, he can draw a new will.

Give the original copy of your will to your attorney or the trust department of your financial institution, keeping only a copy in your home file. Do not store the original in your safe-deposit box; the box may be sealed at your death, causing difficulties in retrieving the will.

Mistakes to Avoid

Drawing wills is a technical skill you should leave to an attorney, but you can help him by being alert to some common pitfalls.

- Don't think you're covered by your spouse's will because you hold property jointly. If you both die together, say in an automobile accident, your jointly owned property might go to probate. If your spouse dies instantly, and you (the beneficiary) die a day later, you die intestate and your combined estates may fall under your state's intestate laws.
- Choose appropriate witnesses to your will. If your will is not executed by proper witnessing at the time you sign it, or it fails to adhere to the strict requirements of state law, your will may be declared invalid. If possible, don't choose witnesses significantly older than you who might die before you.
- Name alternate beneficiaries for specific gifts in case the primary beneficiary dies before you.
- Remember that your beneficiary—not your estate—pays taxes on your gift. You won't benefit the recipient of your Rolls-Royce if he has to sell it to pay the taxes on it. You can, however, shift the tax burden in several ways through proper planning.
- To avoid tax misunderstandings, ask the beneficiary of a gift to sign a dated receipt that describes it.
- If you want to exclude a spouse or child from your will, you must specifically state that. A spouse or child not mentioned in a will is called

a pretermitted heir. Because the law protects them from the oversight of the person writing the will, they have legal recourse unless they are specifically excluded in the will.

EXECUTORS AND TRUSTEES

Executors. You name an executor in your will to carry out its instructions. What your executor does is gather information about estate assets and liabilities, act as caretaker of those assets during probate, keep accurate records of transactions, and distribute the assets of your estate.

An executor also has investment responsibilities—for instance, preserving your property during probate and selecting the assets needed to pay taxes and other expenses of the estate. The job is time-consuming but temporary; it normally lasts from nine months to a year and a half.

For your executor, consider a close family member, an astute friend, a trusted professional, such as your attorney or accountant, or the trust department of your bank or other financial institution. Since the executor can be held personally responsible for errors, you may prefer to use a professional or a financial institution.

Naturally, make sure the person you choose understands the responsibilities and agrees to take them on. It's also a good idea to name a successor executor in case your first choice becomes unwilling or unable to serve.

Fees for executors are normally set by state, not federal, law, although it's sometimes possible to agree on a fee with your executor before your death.

Trustees. People often confuse trustees and executors. Your trustee administers whatever part of your estate you placed in a trust; your executor administers your assets that are subject to probate. The trustee's job lasts for the life of the trust, which can be many years; the executor is through once your estate is settled.

Your trustee's main job is to make prudent investments that protect your beneficiaries. Each state has laws that govern trustees and hold them accountable to the beneficiaries of the trust.

Whether you select a financial institution, a professional investment advisor, or an individual to be your one trustee, be certain they are skilled at managing money.

When you name your trustee, also name a successor trustee in case your initial choice for any reason cannot or will not serve.

Fees for trustees are not set by law. The trust department of a financial institution will normally charge a set annual fee or a percentage of the trust's assets. An individual trustee will charge whatever you agree on in advance, or, without a prior agreement, a reasonable amount set by the probate court.

When you interview prospective candidates, use the evaluation guides at the end of the book. *Evaluation Guide: Individual Executor or Trustee* (#32) lists the important qualities you should look for in an individual executor and trustee. *Evaluation Guide: Institutional Executor or Trustee* (#33) focuses on an institution's desirable strengths.

PROBATE

Probate is a legal term that can cause the calmest people to throw their hands up in despair. Technically, probate is a court procedure intended to change legal ownership of your property after your death, ensure that your will is valid and your assets are distributed to the people you name, and pay all debts against your estate. So why is probate so chilling?

- Probate can be tedious and frustrating, worse in some states than in others, and can drag on for months and even years.
- Probate is expensive. Your estate has to bear the cost of lawyers, accountants, appraisers, and the executor.
- Wills passed through probate become a matter of public record, available for anyone to read. Such public scrutiny may embarrass your heirs.

If you can plan your estate to avoid probate, your heirs will bless you.

How to Avoid Probate

Certain assets don't have to go through a will and, therefore, are not subject to probate administration:

- Assets held in joint tenancy and assets placed in a trust.
- The proceeds from your life insurance policy, which will go directly to the person or trust you name as your beneficiary.
- Most U.S. Savings Bonds, which go directly to the person listed on the face of the bond, if you haven't specified otherwise in your will.

There's also an alternative to the drawbacks of probate: Establish a revocable living trust, described in the preceding chapter.

CHILDPROOF: PROTECTING YOUR CHILD

10

"What would happen to your children if you were killed in an accident?" we abruptly asked a couple we were having dinner with. This is a topic that's been on our minds since our friends' car accident.

Elaine laughed. "'They'd probably watch MTV all day." But Len rolled his eyes—we had obviously hit a raw nerve.

"When we first made out our wills, my brother was married and starting a family right near us, so without even discussing it with him, we named him guardian," said Len. "We thought we were set, but he just got divorced, and he's living a bachelor's life—and loving it. We probably ought to find another guardian."

Elaine took up their story. "My sister, who's ten years younger than I am, certainly isn't capable of being a guardian to our children. And our parents are too old. We just don't know what to do," she said.

"Actually, we're thinking about our best friends—even though they live two thousand miles away—because they're just the best parents we know," she added. "It's awesome to assign this job to your friends, but we decided we'd rather have them than family. It wasn't an easy choice."

Elaine's right. It isn't an easy choice, but it's probably the most important one you'll ever make for your family. Curiously, most people make it haphazardly, and some people don't make it at all.

Even though parents spend a lot of time boasting about their children's exploits or moaning over their falls from favor or bicycles, most couples really don't spend enough time carefully planning for the fundamental well-being of their children. Very few think through that big question: What if a tragedy strikes and your children are orphaned?

There are a host of ramifications beyond the main choice of who will be in charge. How do your children feel about their new guardian? If the guardian lives elsewhere, as is likely, how will the kids feel about moving away? If you've chosen someone outside your family, how will your siblings and, more to the point, your parents, feel about it? In fact, how will your children feel about joining another family when they still have close relatives of their own? As Elaine said, it isn't easy.

Add to all this the increasingly common disruptions in family life: Grandparents move to the Sunbelt, far from children and grandchildren. Even if Grandma does live nearby, chances are she has a full life, perhaps even a full-time job of her own. In today's world, where divorce is frequent and cross-country job transfers almost as regular as commuter trains, very little stays the same. And the one thing we parents want for our children is stability and continuity.

Frankly, that's why we're dumbfounded when parents—and that includes many single parents—say, "The kids will be all right. After all, we have enough life insurance, cash in the bank, and a will."

What we've learned from many parents is that there's a lot more to protecting your offspring than money and a will. For example, even with the most trustworthy and thoughtfully chosen guardian, a host of problems can arise after one or both parents dies. Consider the following scenarios:

- The guardian you named dies and, because you failed to designate a successor guardian, the state appoints a new one.
- You place the bulk of your child's inheritance in an ironclad trust that can't be touched until he reaches a certain age; before that time his needs change dramatically, creating major financial problems for him.
- Your child receives the money you intended, but loses it through poor money management or divorce.

Naturally, you can't anticipate your child's future, but as caring parents you can try to guard against a variety of circumstances, foreseen and unforeseen, in your estate planning. Sadly, this is an area many parents overlook, perhaps because until now information has been sparse.

Good "childproofing" touches several issues: special provisions in your will and/or trusts, guardians, trustees, and—just as important for your child as for you—educating your child to financial matters.

WILLS AND TRUSTS

Since a will is the basis of sensible estate planning, we urge you to review yours at least once a year (see Chapter 8, Planning Your Estate). For the sake of your offspring, keep the following questions in mind during your review:

- Have any of your child's needs changed since the will or trust was drafted?
- Are the guardians, executors, and trustees still willing and able to serve,

or have any of them moved away, died, grown old, or in any other way become unsuitable?

● Have the tax laws relating to your children changed since the original will or trust was drafted?

● Are the provisions for distributing funds to your child still appropriate?

Handling Big Bucks

You know how well your children handle money, but if they are typical, they probably can't handle large sums responsibly until they are at least close to thirty. We've heard many a parent complain that funds distributed before then are often dissipated.

Moreover, with the high rate of divorce, you have to face the possibility that your child will be divorced. If your inheritance becomes part of the divorce settlement, it's lost forever, and your intent to provide for your child is lost with it.

For this reason, consider making partial distributions as your child reaches various ages: perhaps one-third at age thirty, one-third at age thirty-five, and the remainder at age forty. Or you could provide a certain level of income until your child reaches a certain age, when the remainder is distributed.

It's hard to foretell the future, but as you review your will and trusts, try to help your children weather potential emergencies. And if you've established a trust, give the trustee leeway to do the same.

GUARDIANS

A guardian is the person you select to raise your child if you die and if your spouse is unable, unqualified, or unwilling to raise your minor child. Normally, when one parent dies, the other parent becomes the guardian. You cannot, by will or otherwise, take this right away without good cause supported in a court of law.

If both parents die, someone must be designated as guardian. If you haven't made arrangements, the state will. As you can see, nominating a guardian is probably the most important provision in your will.

Types of Guardians

There are two kinds of guardians: guardians of the person, and guardians of the estate. And although most parents nominate the same person for both, the responsibilities are quite different.

The *guardian of the person* is responsible for the care, custody, and control of your child's daily life—and that includes food, clothing, and education. This person determines where the child will live and can authorize medical treatment. Naturally, you also want the guardian to provide the love and attention your child would otherwise receive from a parent. You may pay these guardians if you wish, but you should, if possible, provide funds for child care.

The *guardian of the estate* handles the business aspects of the relationship, including investing and managing the child's estate. When your child's assets involve complex financial decisions, you have good reason to choose a separate guardian of the estate. In many cases, the size of your estate will determine whether this special expertise is necessary. You customarily pay a fee for this service, either a flat fee or a percentage of the estate.

Selecting a Guardian

As you choose a stand-in for your most personal role—that of parent—you naturally seek a replacement who will be as caring, understanding, prudent, wise, and wonderful with your children as you are. To aid your search, two worksheets—*Evaluation Guide: Guardian of the Person* (#34) and *Evaluation Guide: Guardian of the Estate* (#35)—focus on the qualities you want for each job.

Also consider the following:

- Does the candidate have the necessary qualities—maturity, experience, temperament, integrity, stability—to be your child's guardian?
- Will a potential guardian understand the emotional needs and problems of your child?
- If you select one set of grandparents as guardians, will they have the stamina and patience for this role? How will the other set of grandparents feel if they're not chosen?
- Have you considered your candidate's age, marital status, other children, and, frankly, stability of the marriage?
- Will a prospective guardian have time for the task? Even if there are already other children? Even if both spouses work?
- Are you providing sufficient funds, or can the candidate take on this extra financial burden?
- Are your children old enough to participate in this decision? Knowing how they will be taken care of and by whom can allay the secret fears of many children.

When you settle on a candidate for guardian, understand that you only *nominate* that person; the court actually appoints the guardian. Nomination does not assure appointment, but it does carry great weight with the judge.

At the same time you choose your nominee, designate an alternate, or successor, guardian in your will in case the original guardian dies or is unwilling or unable to serve.

Professional Guardian of the Estate

If you feel uneasy turning over your child's estate to an individual, you can appoint a professional or corporate guardian of the estate, such as an accountant, lawyer, or the trust department of a bank. Normally, fees are based on a percentage of the market value of the estate or of the annual income.

Common Pitfalls in Choosing Guardians

- Parents don't consult with prospective guardians before naming them.
- Each parent nominates a different guardian (generally a member of that person's immediate family) in his or her will, which creates a tremendous problem for the court. Disputes burgeon if the parents are divorced.
- You choose co-guardians, commonly a husband and wife. This is appealing, but it raises problems if there is a subsequent divorce, separation, or death. In that case, the surviving guardian is responsible alone.
- You fail to provide for particular problems, such as medical or hospital care, that you know will occur.
- You aren't sensitive to whether the guardian can afford similar financial support for his children that you are providing him to spend on your children, and whether that difference in life-style will upset the guardian's household. You can remedy potential distress by offering to provide similar financial assistance to the guardian's own children.

Mandatory Guardians

If your children are old enough to take care of themselves but have not yet reached their legal majority, you may feel they don't need a legal guardian. However, there are circumstances where a guardian is mandatory. Here again, if you haven't selected one, the court will.

Some common situations that require a guardian are:

- When your child becomes a beneficiary under an insurance policy. (Most insurance companies won't pay benefits without a guardian of the estate.)
- If your child receives property under any kind of property settlement.
- If any liability claim is made against your child.

Guardianships of the Estate vs. Trusts

Before you settle on a guardian of the estate, consider the use of a trust instead. Ask an estate lawyer if a trust is a good idea for you. Meanwhile, here are some of the benefits.

- You can establish a single trust for all of your children; you need a separate guardianship for each minor child.
- With a trust you can set up a family "pot" to meet heavy expenses such as medical care for any child; with separate guardianships, you must divide your funds among them and hope that one child doesn't exhaust his or her fund.
- The guardianship of the estate of a minor child terminates by law when the child reaches majority. With a trust, you can postpone termination beyond legal majority, even until, if you choose, your child's death.
- If you are considering a trust, use the *Trustee Evaluation Guide* (#36) to assess potential trustees.

Once you've settled on your choice of guardians and trustees, list them on the *Childproof Protection Summary* (#37), together with the provisions you've made for each child in your will. As with all the worksheets, keep this summary up to date.

FINANCIAL GIFT-GIVING

One good way to begin to shift property from your estate to your children's is by giving them gifts. This removes those assets from your estate so they aren't taxed at your death and also lowers your own annual tax bill.

Each year, each parent can give each child a maximum sum without incurring any federal gift tax; the gift can be $10,000 a year, or $20,000 per couple. Moreover, you aren't limited to cash; you can also transfer securities. When these are sold, the profits will be taxed at capital gains rates and not as ordinary income.

If you want to encourage older children who work full-time to start IRAs, make your financial gift a full or partial contribution to it. Your children can take that IRA contribution as a tax deduction from their incomes—an immediate benefit to them.

HELP YOUR KIDS BE FINANCIALLY SAVVY

Handling money doesn't come naturally, and when children receive large sums through wills or trusts, most of them aren't prepared to manage their funds. It's your responsibility to give them a basic understanding of finances and of money as a tool. They'll appreciate soon enough the hard work it takes to make it. An excellent start is to include your children in the financial decisions that affect them.

Allowances

An allowance is a good step in your child's financial education. "Regular spending money is a preferable way to meet a child's needs, both his practical need for money and his emotional need for independence," says financial expert Grace W. Weinstein, author of *Children and Money*.

When you give your child a fixed amount—no strings attached—you give him the opportunity to make independent choices (both good and bad ones) and the chance to manage or mismanage his resources. An allowance teaches a basic financial lesson: If your child doesn't handle his money well, he'll run out. For your part, if your child exhausts funds before the next pay day, don't bail him out.

If your child regularly runs out of money, review the amount periodically, perhaps during a family budget session. Be sure it meets his needs, and agree on what it is to cover. And don't tie the allowance to your child's behavior.

Children and Work

In place of an allowance, or in addition to one, you may want to pay your child for performing specific household chores. Try to distinguish between daily tasks that you expect each family member to perform, such as picking up one's clothes, making one's bed, or putting out the garbage, and jobs for which you would otherwise hire outside help, such as cleaning the windows or washing the car. Our oldest daughter is glad for the clarification. She knows we expect her to wash the family dishes, but as soon as we have company, she's free to charge for her clean-up services—and she does.

By the time your children are in their teens we believe they should work part-time—and not at home. "The surest road to independence, to an understanding of real work and real earnings, is through work outside the home," says Weinstein. Whether it's baby-sitting, gardening for neighbors, working in a fast-food restaurant or retail store, or helping in the family business, children learn the meaning of work and money best at firsthand.

Bank Accounts

Start with at least a savings account, but, if possible, set up both savings and checking accounts for your children while they're in their teens. They'll learn to balance their own checkbooks early and may pick up a savings habit.

Credit Cards, Pro and Con

Credit cards are too hard for youngsters to handle, but some department stores are issuing charge (not credit) cards to teenagers. These have nominal credit limits and/or require a parent to co-sign; either way, parents are ultimately responsible for the purchases. A credit card of one's own—with built-in brakes—may teach one youngster good buying habits and responsibility for consumer behavior, but it can lure another into a buying spree. Know your child before you offer a credit card.

THE ROLE OF LIFE INSURANCE

11

For most people, buying life insurance ranks right up there with death and taxes: the insurance reminds them all too much of the former, and the premiums come with the regularity of the latter. They think—mistakenly—that life insurance is expensive and complicated to buy. And they can't figure out how much they need. That's why many couples, especially young ones, would rather operate on what we call the blue sky theory: Why carry life insurance? Nothing's going to rain on our parade.

That was how Carol, a young widow we met in Chicago, felt—until the sky fell in and she was drowning in the deluge. "When you're in your twenties and thirties, you don't think seriously of buying life insurance," she said. "You think, 'My God, we have all those years ahead.'" When her husband, Bud, died of a heart attack in his office, Carol had a twelve-year-old daughter, no job, and no life insurance benefits to cushion the blow. She had to sell their suburban house and move back with her parents until she found work and a small apartment. "It was tough that first year," she said softly.

Another couple in New York really validated our blue sky theory. Even though Peter had Hodgkin's disease virtually all through his ten-year marriage to Sally, they never considered life insurance.

"It was weird. It never entered my mind that anything would really happen," said Sally. "Even though we had children, life insurance was an expense we felt we just couldn't afford. When Peter's health began to fail seriously and he tried desperately to buy some, he couldn't get any," she added bitterly.

That's the way it is with life insurance (and most other kinds, too). Just when you need it the most, it's the hardest to get. If you have a policy and don't pay the premiums, the results are even harder to take, as one Los Angeles couple learned.

Vicki and Fred owned a real estate agency. Several years ago when they were short of funds, they let their one insurance policy lapse. Before they got around to buying another policy, Fred was diagnosed with terminal cancer. During the two years before Fred died, Vicki frantically tried to get insurance. She couldn't because Fred was "uninsurable." Then she heard about "open enrollment" policies, sometimes a way to buy life insurance without a medical examination, which we'll explain later.

"I picked up whatever open enrollments came my way, which is perfectly legal," she said. "That was the only kind of policy we could secure. It wasn't much coverage, but it took care of the bills those first few months."

Scrimping on life insurance is a common mistake of many young couples. It's too bad, because there isn't a less expensive way to safeguard your assets and prevent loss of income. Life insurance is actually among the best buys you can make. It creates cash, and it can generate an income for you for whatever length of time you choose. For example, a forty-two-year-old systems manager we know is buying $1 million worth of protection for his family for less than $1,500 a year.

After you read in this chapter about the different types of insurance, and how to figure how much you need, review your family's life insurance program to see if it will meet your needs. Too many of us find out too late that life without adequate insurance is very hard indeed.

HOW MUCH INSURANCE DO YOU NEED?

That's always the big question. Most people feel they can't answer it without a crystal ball, but in fact you can make a sound educated estimate by using the *Life Insurance Worksheet* (#38) in the Workbook section of this book. This worksheet highlights your family's continuing financial requirements and suggests a formula to determine how much insurance you need.

First, estimate your immediate cash needs in the event of your spouse's death. Would you have any debts to pay? Medical bills that wouldn't be covered by insurance or by your major medical deductible? Any other sizable amounts to disburse?

You'll want an emergency fund, and that amount is always difficult to project. The easiest way is simply to select a figure as a cushion, perhaps your living expenses for a year.

You also need to anticipate how much money, if any, you may need for federal or state inheritance taxes. Although the new federal laws will eliminate this for spouses, if you and your spouse are in a fatal accident, your joint deaths may cause a tax problem for your dependents.

Second, figure your long-term cash needs. These will depend on the long-range financial plans you have already made, but don't forget that you still may want to create a retirement income, a savings income, and special funds for college or other family needs.

Third, calculate your monthly cash needs, using your budget worksheets

(#s 23–27). You know how much money you need today. How much monthly income do you want to provide for dependents? For any other household expenses? Use your best guess to determine those immediate future needs. Then multiply your estimated monthly budget by the length of time you want to cover.

Note: In estimating your loss of income, plan to replace at least 75 percent of it.

When you total your immediate cash requirements, your family's long-term needs, and the income for the monthly cash needs, you'll have a reliable idea of how much money you want to leave. You don't have to cover the entire amount with life insurance if you have other assets. To see how much your assets can reduce your life insurance needs, review Chapter 3, Figuring Your Net Worth, and worksheets #14 and #15.

In addition to providing for living expenses, you might also want to set up monthly allowances for your dependents, or give them each one lump sum. The place to list that is on the *Dependent Income Worksheet* (#39).

While you're reviewing your family's future cash needs, take the time to consider how much money and what specific assets you want to leave other people; note this on the *Beneficiary Worksheet* (#40). By correlating this information with your life insurance calculations, you can see if you're carrying sufficient insurance to do what you want to. This worksheet will also be helpful in preparing your will (see Chapter 9, Distributing Your Assets), and, needless to say, it should jibe with your *Will Preparation Worksheet* (#30).

WHAT KIND OF LIFE INSURANCE SHOULD YOU BUY?

There are several types of life insurance and various ways to buy them, so understanding your options will give you better coverage and probably at better prices. As you shop for insurance, keep the differences in mind.

Term Insurance

Term insurance lasts for a specified period of time, or "term"; it usually runs for one, five, ten years, or until a specified age, such as sixty-five. Its principal benefit is that it is the least expensive type of individual life insurance. Term insurance pays only on the death of the insured person and does not build up any cash value. Be wary of some term policies, known as decreasing term policies, that will reduce the amount of insurance annually; they cost less than level term policies.

A conversion clause in the policy is equally important. This lets you convert your term policy to a permanent (ordinary, straight, or whole) life policy without a physical exam, and is particularly attractive as you reach age sixty and term insurance becomes very expensive.

If possible, include a renewable clause that lets you extend your policy for additional term periods without a medical examination. Your premium will change (it's based on age), but at least you'll be able to maintain insurance even if your health fails.

Permanent Life Policies (Ordinary, Whole, or Straight)

This type of policy guarantees you coverage for as long as you live. The amount of insurance is normally at least the original face value, minus any loans against the policy. Unlike term insurance, permanent life insurance builds up a cash value over the years so that whenever you cancel your policy, you will receive the cash value that has accumulated. Moreover, you can use that cash value to pay your insurance premiums, borrow money from the insurance company at a guaranteed favorable interest rate, or as retirement income.

Because of the benefits of ordinary life insurance, its premiums are higher than those for term insurance. Its ultimate cost, however, may or may not be more, depending on how long you keep it and when you die. Some ordinary life policies also pay dividends that you can use to increase the amount of your insurance or reduce your next premium payment.

Universal Life Policies (Adjustable or Variable Premium)

Within broad limits, this type of insurance lets you determine the amount of your annual premiums. The portion of the premium above the cost of term insurance for each year is invested by the life insurance company and generates income, which stays in the policy and increases its cash value. You can withdraw these earnings and not pay taxes on them until the amount you withdraw exceeds the premiums you paid over the life of the insurance policy. You can raise or lower the face amount of the policy, which also changes the premiums.

Moreover, all along you receive interest on the cash value as it accrues in the policy, just as you would in a whole life policy; the rate varies with the insurance company. This "right" to redesign your policy each year lets you adapt your premiums and benefits to your ever-changing circumstances.

Group Life Insurance

Most employers now make group life insurance available for their employees, and pay part or all of the premium.

The first $50,000 of group life insurance is income tax free to you, but you pay a tax on higher levels of coverage. You may be better off buying individual life insurance if you want more coverage.

Group insurance is a nice supplement to your life insurance program, but it has its limitations: the coverage may be low, there is no cash value build-up, it stops when you change employers, and if it's not subsidized by your employer, it may cost more than individual coverage if you're younger than forty-five to fifty.

Open Enrollment

This is a form of group life insurance that some companies advertise in newspapers and trade magazines. You can purchase a few of these policies by mail without having a medical examination, although most programs require you to complete a brief medical questionnaire. The premiums vary with each plan, but are normally slightly higher than standard insurance programs.

Different groups, institutions, or associations offer open enrollment insurance policies to the public at certain "open" times. This is perfectly legal.

They can also be a life saver, as Vicki discovered. "When I was looking for open enrollments, I became an avid junk mail reader," she said. "I picked up one policy from a savings-and-loan association during a thirty-day open enrollment and another one that my stock brokerage house offered its clients with cash fund accounts."

The insurance companies expect people with urgent short-term needs to take advantage of the opportunity, so they often attach some strings. For example, a $100,000 policy might only pay $5,000 the first year, $15,000 the second year, $25,000 the third year, and not pay the full $100,000 until the fourth year. But as Vicki pointed out, "Even with the premiums, you'd probably come out ahead the first year. Five thousand dollars would pay some big bills."

SOME BUYING TIPS FOR LIFE INSURANCE

Changes in the insurance industry are rapid and sometimes dramatic these days. A good life insurance agent can give you current information. (See Chapter 2, Picking Your Advisory Team, for advice on choosing a good agent.)

- Select an insurance company whose policy meets your specific needs. However, if it's not a major, well-known company, check its standing with your State Department of Insurance or review its rating in *Best's Insurance Guide* (in your local library).
- Review all the life policies that you bought four or more years ago; the cost of life insurance has dropped dramatically and you may be able to find substantial savings.
- Also, review how you pay your premiums. Most insurance companies charge interest if you pay monthly or quarterly, rather than annually. Monthly "preauthorized check payments" (PAC) through your checking account can give you the ease of monthly payments without substantially increasing your costs. The charge for PAC varies with each company, but it's usually less than all payment methods, other than the single annual premium.
- Contrary to popular belief, almost everyone can get life insurance. Obviously, your premiums will reflect the state of your health, but you'll always find insurance companies that provide nonstandard life insurance coverage, even though it may be at higher rates for greater health

risks. These surcharged premiums will drop when your medical condition improves.

- *Never cancel an existing policy until you know you can obtain a new policy elsewhere.*

PLANNING AHEAD: HOW TO HANDLE LIFE INSURANCE PAYOUTS

Normally, the proceeds of any life insurance policy are large sums. And they can present problems—and opportunities—in planning for their disbursement, particularly in how they are paid out, and in how they are taxed.

You can have life insurance beneficiary payments made in several ways:

- The insurance company can hold the proceeds and, for a specified period, only pay interest on it. This is called the *interest income* method.
- Payments can be made on a pre-determined schedule at a pre-determined rate. This is called *income for a specified period*.
- Payments can be made for the life of the beneficiary or beneficiaries jointly. This is called the *life income method*.

A word of caution when using any of these payment options: What seems like a good idea today may not be the best arrangement for your beneficiaries tomorrow. Consider the consequences carefully before designating any one plan.

ARE YOU MAKING THESE COMMON MISTAKES?

Putting your life insurance in your safe-deposit box? In many states, that box is sealed at a death, and entry is time-consuming and tedious. Keep insurance policies in your home file so you can turn them in promptly for settlement. If you misplace them, get a copy from your insurance company.

Not naming specific beneficiaries? A general statement, like "children of this marriage," won't do. If you don't clearly designate your beneficiaries, you may delay settlement of life insurance claims. A broad, but specific, description is best, such as: "All natural and adopted children, plus any daughter of my spouse." Whenever your family status changes—say you have additional children or a family member dies—update those changes on your insurance policy. Also, be sure your designation of life insurance beneficiaries agrees with the provisions in your will.

Naming your estate as beneficiary? This raises the value of your estate because the proceeds become cash. They not only increase estate taxes, but also become subject to claims against the estate. You can avoid this by establishing a life insurance trust, which pays all life insurance benefits outside of your taxable estate. An insurance trust gives you all the normal benefits of your life insurance without any of the tax disadvantages.

Not insuring the wife? Husbands rarely consider the impact on family finances should their wives die. With working wives, it's the loss of a second income. If the wife doesn't earn money, there will be the cost of replacing her services to the family. Income taxes will increase because the family can no longer file a joint income tax return.

Designating the wrong owner? The owner of a life insurance policy is the person responsible for paying the premiums, and not necessarily the one who is insured. There are tax advantages to naming the beneficiary as the owner (the proceeds won't be part of your estate), but that can make it difficult for you to change provisions under the policy without the approval of the owner, and it gives the owner control over any policy loans or cancellation rights.

Relying too heavily on your employer's group insurance? When you leave that employer, you normally have thirty days to convert from the group to an individual policy, even though you may have become uninsurable. However, that conversion policy is expensive; the insurance company realizes that if you didn't have health problems, you would take a medical exam and get new insurance at a lower cost.

Buying additional insurance through your employer's group plan? Most employers furnish life insurance to their employees through a group insurance program. These group plans may also let you buy additional life insurance at your own expense. Normally, this is a poor purchase because the premium you will pay for the added insurance is higher than if you bought that extra insurance as an individual.

No "waiver of premium" clause? This clause forgives all future premium payments and keeps your life insurance policy in force if you become totally and permanently disabled. Adding this coverage to your policy isn't expensive.

Buying the accidental death benefit? This clause, sometimes called "double indemnity," pays double the life insurance benefit if your death is caused by accident. If you need greater amounts of coverage, you shouldn't depend on an accident to provide them. Moreover, the additional premium isn't cost effective.

Picking the wrong insurance company? The size and visibility of life insurance companies don't necessarily determine their financial stability or competitive policies. The cost of life insurance varies dramatically from company to company. Consult your life insurance agent, your State Department of Insurance, or *Best's Insurance Guide,* which rates companies on their financial stability and the quality of their management and is available at most local libraries.

Not reviewing your life insurance program regularly? Inflation and changes in health and family relationships all bear on your insurance needs. Make sure your policies keep pace with the rest of your life.

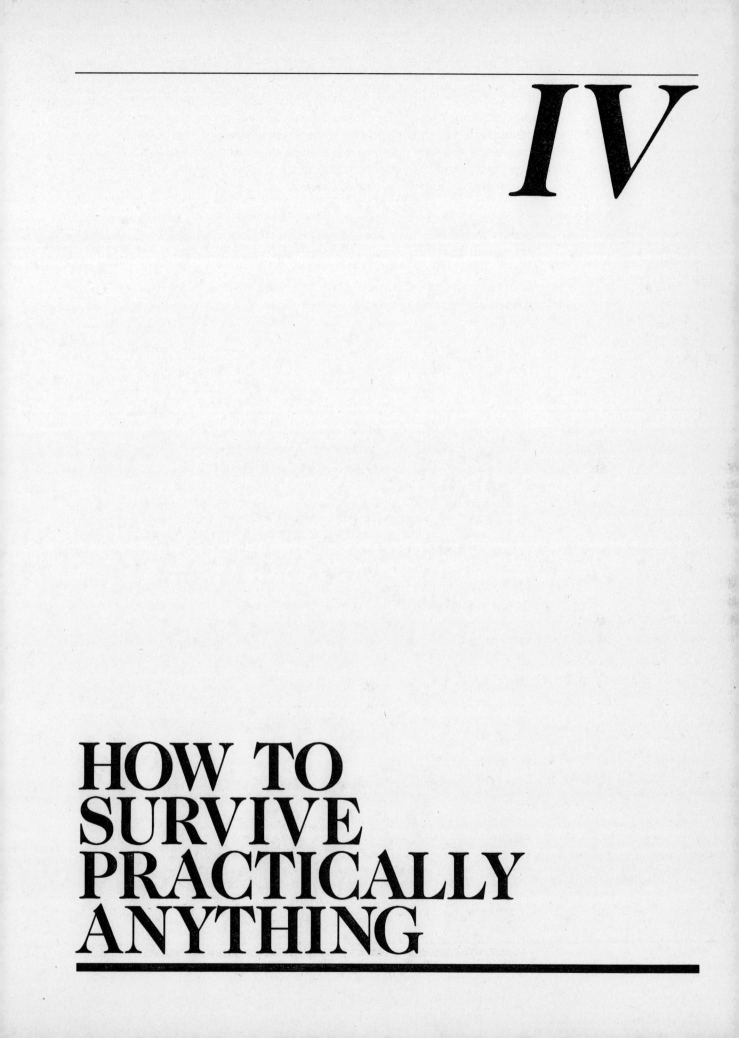

IV

HOW TO SURVIVE PRACTICALLY ANYTHING

SERIOUS ILLNESS

12

Practically everybody has health insurance, but hardly anyone knows exactly what's in the policy. That can be perilous. Time and again we heard horror stories from people who assumed—mistakenly—that their families were covered under particular circumstances. Occasionally we spoke to someone who happened to be lucky.

Karen, a suburban Detroit grandmother, was one of the fortunate few. "We had taken out health insurance when we were first married, and never bothered to think about it again until Joe got sick," she said. "It had a $30,000 limit and a semi-private room rate of $20 a day. You can imagine how far that would go! At the time he got sick, the semi-private rate was $80 a day—and now it's in the hundreds."

Karen shook her head in disbelief. "It never occurred to us to ask the agent if our medical insurance needed updating," she said. "But by dumb luck, a month before Joe got sick he joined a group plan, which carried him through his illness. If we hadn't had that new coverage, I would have been in deep, deep trouble."

A family we met in Virginia wasn't as lucky. Tim is a salesman who changed jobs shortly before June's ulcer flared up. To their dismay, they discovered that Tim's new health insurance didn't cover a "pre-existing condition." They had to foot the bill for June's ulcer alone.

As if that wasn't bad enough, when Tim had a slight stroke several years later and was sent to a nursing home for physical therapy, the policy didn't cover that either. "It paid the doctors," June explained, "but because Tim hadn't been in a hospital for ten days before he was admitted to the nursing home, the insurance company wouldn't pick up the cost of the therapy."

Tim and June have since bought supplementary insurance, but it was expensive—and frightening—to find big gaps in their coverage. As June said, "You never know what surprises you'll find in your policy until you go to use it."

We sympathized with June, but we didn't tell her she was dead wrong. Insurance is one place you don't want to be surprised. As you can see, it's essential to know—and understand—your health insurance coverage *before* you use it.

Even if you know exactly what's in your policy, the cost of a long illness can be overwhelming. Vicki and Fred, the owners of a real estate agency, had a good family major medical policy that covered 80 percent of the costs. "When Fred was first diagnosed with terminal cancer, he spent a month in the hospital. The bill was something like $50,000," said Vicki. "Even though we only paid 20 percent up to a certain amount, it was very costly for us. I could see that if Fred had to go into the hospital again, I could run through my life savings in a hurry."

Vicki was savvy enough to learn about open enrollments—insurance you can get without a medical examination. When she bought some life insurance through a trade association, she discovered she could also get medical insurance the same way. Fred joined a fraternal organization for its open enrollment medical policy.

"We felt a little guilty about that," she said, "and we called the organization and told them what we were doing, but they said it was perfectly legal. Evidently, insurance companies figure on picking up people like us who need the coverage."

As you can see, there are usually ways to solve even the bleakest health insurance problems. But you'll avoid some agonizing moments and keep your costs in line if you have the right answers to these questions:

- Does your medical insurance keep pace with the rising cost of health care?
- Have you reviewed your coverage against prevailing doctors' fees and medical costs?
- Do you know how to cover yourself when you're between jobs? When you're self-employed?
- Should you and your spouse each have a group policy?
- What happens to your medical insurance if you're covered under your spouse's policy and he or she dies?
- In fact, do you even know how to analyze a health insurance policy?

We know this is a confusing field. Health insurance, with its wide range of coverage offering an array of choices, is far more complex than any other type of insurance you're likely to buy. It covers you in two major areas: medical expenses and disability income. In this chapter we'll review medical expense insurance; we'll talk about disability in the following one.

TYPES OF MEDICAL EXPENSE INSURANCE

You know that, in general, medical expense insurance potentially covers all your health needs, but when you review your specific insurance, it helps to understand that you can buy protection in eight major areas: basic medical care; basic surgical services; basic hospital expenses; hospital confinement coverage; major medical costs; Medicare supplement; accidents; and specific diseases. You may not want to buy coverage in every area, but you do want to know the impact of each kind.

Basic medical care. This covers your physician's costs for diagnosis and treatment of illness, including prescription drugs, X-rays, lab tests, and other services.

Basic surgical services. This pays a physician's fees whether he performs the surgery in or out of a hospital. Normally the policy includes a surgical schedule listing the maximum amount paid for each type of surgical procedure. In most cases, office visits directly related to the surgery will be covered on a limited basis.

Basic hospital expense. This covers your daily room and care, hospital supplies, and general services, such as X-rays, medications, and laboratory tests while you're an inpatient, with different limitations, depending on your policy. Some of the variables are length of a continuous hospital stay (usually from thirty days to one year), maximum benefit for each injury or illness, room allowance (semi-private or a maximum room rate), and miscellaneous expenses (normally limited to twenty times the daily room rate).

The basic medical, surgical, and hospital expense policies have a deductible amount that you must pay before your insurance coverage begins. The deductible, which may vary from $50 to $500, is applied each year against the expenses of each individual on the policy or, preferably, against the entire family's total expenses.

Hospital confinement coverage. This pays you a specified sum every day, week, or month you're in a hospital, with no limitations on how you use the money. These policies are normally sold by direct mail and supplement your primary health insurance policy.

Major medical. This is by far the most important insurance because it, more than any other kind, protects you against catastrophic loss from a major illness or serious accident. Its maximum coverage ranges from $50,000 to $1 million or more; at least $250,000 is advisable. If you buy less than $1 million, it's imperative that your coverage includes a clause for annual restoration of benefits so the amount of coverage isn't exhausted because of one claim.

Major medical always has a deductible; the higher it is, the lower the cost of the insurance. The deductible can be applied against each individual or, preferably, against the family's collective expenses.

Some policies specify a calendar-year benefit, in which you are reimbursed only for bills submitted during that year; if your illness carries into the next calendar year, a new deductible would apply. Other policies have a "per condition" clause in which benefits are not limited to a specific period of time.

Normally, major medical has a "co-insurance" feature that requires you to share the cost, usually 20 percent, with the insurance company. Some companies offer a "stop-loss" provision, which puts a ceiling, say $1,000 or $2,000, on your annual medical costs, after which the insurance company pays 100 percent of your bills (up to your maximum coverage).

Medicare supplement. This begins when Medicare payments stop. You are eligible for Medicare at any age if you have been entitled to Social Security disability benefits for two years.

Accident only coverage. As its name implies, this coverage protects you for an accident and not a sickness. Normally it covers all family members to the limit you select.

Specified disease coverage. This protects you against one or more named catastrophic diseases, such as cancer or heart problems, with a maximum amount for each disease.

It is possible—and quite common—to purchase these coverages in combination, such as basic coverage plus major medical, or basic coverage plus surgical services.

HOW DOES YOUR HEALTH INSURANCE RATE?

To see how adequate your existing medical coverage is, review it—and any policies you are considering—against the following questions. Record your findings on the *Medical Insurance Coverage Worksheet* (#41) at the end of the book. To see if you're getting the best buy for your insurance buck, complete the *Medical Insurance Cost/Coverage Comparison* (#42) worksheet.

Is there a "pre-existing condition" clause? This means that you would not be covered for any health problems you or your family had before the policy became effective. Sometimes you can have this clause waived by taking a physical exam that shows the condition hasn't existed for a period of time.

What is the maximum coverage your major medical policy provides? Is it for each illness, or is it cumulative for one year or over your lifetime. Is it for each family member, or for the family as a whole? If you can't get at least $250,000 in maximum coverage, consider an excess major medical policy with significantly higher limits. Since a serious illness can run daily hospital costs over $3,000, even that limit wouldn't cover you for three months.

What is the deductible amount you must pay before your coverage begins? Does it apply to each individual, or to the family as a whole? Does it apply to each new claim, or is it based on an annual calender year regardless how many claims you make in that year? You're better off if the deductible is applied once annually to the collective family's expenses and not against each person and each new claim because you would save money by paying fewer deductibles.

How does your policy define "dependent coverage"? Some policies insure all your children, including those away at school, or not living at home, while others restrict coverage to a certain age, usually eighteen or twenty-one. In most cases, your parents who reside with you are not eligible as dependents.

Is nursing care included? This would cover private duty nurses in a hospital when they are prescribed by a doctor. Sometimes that benefit carries over to post-hospital recovery at home.

Are nursing homes covered? Under what conditions? Can a patient go from home to a nursing home without a hospital stay?

Are you covered for maternity benefits? For any complications from a pregnancy?

Is there a "prevailing rate" clause for surgical fees? Are reimbursements geared to the customary doctor's fees in your area, or to a uniform rate? If you live in an expensive area, you want a surgical schedule that keeps pace with the higher fees you will probably be charged. If your policy is out of date, the insurance may not cover your doctors' bills.

Is there a rating formula that relates hospital costs to other expenses? The rating formula is normally one to three times the daily hospital rate; the higher the rate, the larger the allowance for other expenses.

Are you reimbursed for a second surgical opinion? Some policies, particularly group plans, now require you to get the advice of a second surgeon before undergoing a major operation. This doctor, approved by the insurance company, does not perform the surgery but warrants that it is necessary.

What does your policy specifically exclude from coverage? Many policies don't cover cosmetic surgery, dental work, or weight control specialists, or other procedures that may be important to you, except as required by a covered accident.

Can you convert your group plan to an individual policy if you leave your employment? Most group policies allow you to convert to an individual or another group plan if you act within thirty days.

What are the cancellation provisions? Some policies are noncancellable no matter what your health is; others are limited to a specific period, often one, two, or three years.

Is there a "guaranteed renewable" clause? This obligates the insurance company to renew the policy, but they can change the premium.

Do you have psychological coverage? This is not standard in a group policy, but can usually be added on an individual basis.

HOW TO BUY INSURANCE

Group Plans

If you're like most people in the United States, you're insured under a group program, either through an employer or as a member of an organization. Either way, you enjoy better insurance rates than you could get with an individual policy.

If you're an employee, your employer will pay anywhere from half to all the insurance premiums for you, but you're sometimes expected to pick up the cost for your dependents.

Since your employer or organization can change your group coverage at any time, review the policy whenever changes are made. Read the group insurance booklet your employer will give you, and contact the personnel department if you have any questions. Use the *Medical Insurance Coverage Worksheet* (#41) and the *Medical Insurance Cost/Coverage Comparison Worksheet* (#42) to monitor key provisions—for example, the exclusions.

If you're insured under an organization's group plan, you pay your share of the premiums, which are set by the insurance company.

If you aren't insurable and you belong to any organizations that have open enrollment periods in which you can buy medical insurance without a medical examination, take advantage of it.

Health Maintenance Organization (HMO)

HMOs are group plans, but they differ from regular group insurance in that they contract with specific doctors and hospitals to provide services to their clients. The doctors belong either to a group practice and offer care in a clinic setting, or to an individual practice association and see patients in their private offices.

Normally, an HMO offers the same coverage as any other group carrier, except for life insurance, which is sometimes part of a group insurance plan.

The advantage of an HMO is that it can usually provide comparable medical care at a lesser cost than you can get otherwise.

However, there are several features that may trouble you. You can't select your own doctor; you are normally assigned physicians by the HMO in your area, usually at one of their approved clinics, and, except in an emergency, you must use their services. This may be a disadvantage, if you travel frequently.

If there is an HMO in your area, your employer is legally obligated to offer you a choice between his group insurance plan and the HMO. Use the *Evaluating HMO and Group Insurance* (#43) worksheet to compare plans.

Individual Medical Insurance

You can buy any of the medical coverages we've described as an individual, either to supplement or replace any group or HMO format. In either case, carefully check what is and what is not covered; individual policies are often more restrictive than group plans. Look particularly at the pre-existing condition clause, cancellation and guaranteed renewable provisions, the surgery schedule, and the daily hospitalization coverage, including the maximum limit per day and the maximum amount for each hospitalization.

When you buy individual insurance, use an insurance agent who takes the time to explain all the details of the policy to you. (Chapter 2, Picking Your Advisory Team, will help you find a good agent.)

Large group insurers such as Blue Cross/Blue Shield also sell individual policies directly. They offer a variety of programs for individuals.

Direct Mail

Many hospital indemnity and accident coverage policies are solicited through direct mail and newspaper advertising. Although their coverage is too limited to use as primary insurance, they can nicely supplement your existing plans, and the premiums are attractively low.

℞ FOR SOME HEALTH INSURANCE PROBLEMS

You're caught between jobs, without any medical coverage at all.
Consider an interim short-term (usually six months) health insurance policy. It will cost more but it's better than nothing.

You're self-employed and not eligible for any group employment policy.
You need individual insurance, which provides essentially the same coverage as a group policy but costs more. Consider your local Blue Cross/Blue Shield, and commercial health insurance agents.

You and your spouse are employed and are each covered by your employers' group plans.
If you are each paying insurance premiums, the one with the most restrictive policy should decline coverage. Two policies don't give you additional benefits other than covering your deductible, which will be less than the duplicate premium.

You're insured under your spouse's group employment policy, and your spouse dies.

Find out if that group policy covers you for a limited period of time after the death, during which you can get group coverage through an organization, or your own individual coverage. If not, get an interim insurance policy until you can arrange long-term health insurance.

A member of your family has a serious, "pre-existing" condition that requires expensive medical care and isn't covered by your regular health insurance.

Join one or more professional, university, or social organizations that offer group health insurance, or apply to Blue Cross/Blue Shield, during one of their "open enrollment" periods. During this time, usually a thirty-day period, you can obtain coverage without a medical examination. This is perfectly legal.

The benefits of your current policy don't begin to meet today's medical costs.

Ask the insurance company to increase the benefits, or buy supplementary coverage. But *never* cancel your present policy, even if it's inadequate, until your replacement coverage is not only in effect, but until the time limit for all "pre-existing conditions" has passed.

Purchase Hospital Confinement Coverage. It's helpful if you are hospitalized for a long time and invaluable if you are uninsurable for any reason.

As you can see, medical coverage is confusing and complicated. The options constantly change, benefits shift. Any misunderstanding about your coverage can have a devastating impact on your family finances. It's vital to your family's health, financial and otherwise, that you continually review your medical insurance.

DISABILITY

13

"When Tim had his stroke, we were so concerned about the medical insurance that we didn't even think about disability," said June, a pleasant woman we met in Virginia. "It was only a slight stroke, thank God, but even so, Tim was hospitalized for a month, and after resting at home, he was in a nursing home for a month for physical therapy. All in all, he didn't work for six months."

June's voice was tight as she recounted those months when she thought her world was collapsing. Her husband, Tim, is a salesman, and a large part of his salary depends on commissions, so there was a sharp loss of income. There was also the anxiety of not knowing if he could ever go back to work. As June reminded us, a salesman needs to be active and articulate, and Tim's stroke initially left him with a bad limp and slurred speech.

"All the regular monthly bills were coming in, and then, during Tim's lengthy recuperation, our new condo required a major plumbing repair and the property tax came due," she said. "The bad part was that I couldn't even go out to work. Tim needed so much help just doing simple things, like eating, that someone had to be with him all the time. It was either me, or hiring someone else—and I was cheaper."

June and Tim had to live on their savings, but eventually Tim recovered completely, and their ordeal was over in six months. A lawyer we know isn't as fortunate. He has Alzheimer's disease. He has limited disability insurance, and so far, his firm has been generous about carrying him. "That's going to stop soon," his wife told us. "I don't know what we're going to do then."

Most of us rarely consider the possibility that an illness or an accident will force us out of work for a significant period. If we're relatively young, we don't think of extended hospital stays, lengthy recuperations, or an inability to return to work for weeks or months, and certainly not forever. If we have good medical coverage, we feel well protected.

The cruel and frightening fact is that at some time many of us will be laid up and unable to go to work. It may be due to a multiple fracture on the ski slopes rather than a disabling illness, but whatever the cause, we may face a serious loss of income. With no paycheck coming in, we will watch our family's assets drain away.

There are two ways to avoid this financial nightmare: disability insurance, and an emergency disability plan. They go hand in hand.

DISABILITY INSURANCE

Disability insurance is protection against loss of income from injury or illness. There are three common ways to be protected: through Social Security, through your employer, and through an individual policy. Also, there are a few states that have disability protection.

Social Security.   No matter how young they are, Social Security provides disability benefits to anyone eligible for retirement benefits. Most people may not be aware they have this protection. Coverage for a permanent disability can begin with the sixth month, as long as you are expected to be disabled for over twelve months and you have certain Social Security work credits.

Although you may be eligible for benefits, there is a high denial rate and a substantial waiting period (often several months) for payments to start. Normally the benefits will not cover all your expenses, but they will supplement your other disability coverage.

State benefits.   Available in a few states, they vary by state and are limited; however, they do supplement other coverage.

Employment benefits.   These can range from a group disability policy to a specified number of sick days with pay. You may also be able to buy individual disability insurance through your employer's group health insurance policy; if so, seriously consider getting it.

Surprisingly, few companies have a formal policy on how many sick days they allow an employee annually. This is not a required benefit; in the absence of a clear policy, be sure to get individual coverage.

If you or your spouse are principals or partners in a business, disability raises another problem. What happens if either of you becomes totally and permanently disabled? How long would the business pay the salary? When would the other partners or owners want to buy you out? On what terms? A disability agreement is just as important as a buy-and-sell agreement is in case of death; work one out before the fact.

Individual disability insurance.   This is offered through a wide variety of plans whose benefits and limitations require study (see discussion below).

We strongly urge you to consider disability insurance if you have none, or review your existing coverage to be sure it's adequate. You should understand the important questions and definitions in this type of insurance, because it's all too common to have a disability policy that's inadequate when you need it.

How to Rate a Disability Policy

The major points in a disability policy are described below. Use them to analyze the policy you have or the one you're considering. Record your findings on the *Disability Insurance Checklist* (#44) worksheet at the end of the book.

How does the plan define disability? Is it the ability to perform your particular job or any job at all?
    Payment of a disability benefit depends on your status as a disabled person. You can be totally disabled, residually disabled, or partially disabled because of an accident or sickness. Each category is covered differently, and it's critical that you understand the difference.

Total disability.   In the newer policies, this means you are substantially unable to continue working at your job. Total disability benefits can cover you for your lifetime even though you are able to work in another field. However, some policies limit coverage to two to five years. For example, Henry is a surgeon; a spinal injury has made him a paraplegic. He receives payments for total disability even though he now teaches medicine.
    Fortunately, Henry updated his disability policy before he had his accident. Under his previous policy he would have had to forfeit disability benefits if he worked in any occupation for which he was reasonably suited by education, training, or experience—in other words, as a teacher or consultant. Many policies don't pay total disability income if you work in *any* occupation. Moreover, some policies still require total in-hospital or in-house confinement to qualify for total disability. Make certain your policy is not that restricted.

Residual disability.   This provides benefits for significant loss of earnings, usually after a period of continuous total disability. Normally you receive benefits as long as your earnings are at least 20 percent to 25 percent below your predisability income. For example, if Henry could teach or consult but no longer operate, or could only work part-time, his income would probably drop substantially more than 25 percent.

Partial disability.   This provides benefits when you can't perform one or more of the important daily duties of your occupation but are capable of some type of work. If Henry can no longer operate but he can still assist as a consultant in the operating room, he would be eligible for partial disability benefits.

Does your disability insurance cover both illness and accidents?

Some policies cover accidents only, which is not enough. You must protect yourself against illness as well. Normally the length of coverage is lifetime for accidents, but a limited number of years (usually five) for illness.

Must you be totally hospitalized or house-bound to receive benefits?

Most policies let you leave the house or hospital for treatment without loss of benefits. You want the least restrictive definition.

How long must you wait before receiving payments?

A normal waiting period is thirty days, but some plans delay six months or a year before paying. Accident policies pay partial disability benefits immediately from the date of the accident.

How long do payments last?

This varies from a specified period of time to a total dollar figure.

What is the maximum monthly, annual, or total benefit?

Most plans range between 50 percent and 75 percent of your income. The payments are tax free, so the buying power is about the same as your previous taxable income.

Will another source of income (earned or unearned) affect your benefits, such as Social Security or Workers Compensation?

A majority of plans allow other sources of income.

If your employer carries this insurance, are the benefits based on your length of service or salary level?

Some plans require a minimum length of service (usually one or two years) or a certain salary level.

Can you convert your coverage to an individual policy if you leave that employment?

Most plans offer this option.

Is the policy guaranteed renewable?

This is an important safeguard if you carry individual disability insurance; if you're part of your employer's plan, you have no control over this feature.

Can you stop paying the insurance premiums while receiving benefit payments?

This normally doesn't cost more, but it's a feature offered by some insurance companies.

Can the rates be raised?

This is important because the cost of your disability insurance could go beyond your range.

Does a disability from a pre-existing condition prevent coverage?

If this limitation exists in your employer's plan, try to have the plan changed, make certain you get your own coverage without this limitation, or try to have the restriction removed by submitting a medical report or taking a new physical exam stating the condition no longer exists.

Is mental illness excluded?

Normally it is. Check the policy for its definition of mental illness.

How long will the survivor—normally the wife and dependent children—have continued coverage?

Usually, they have ninety days.

If there are any limitations in your employer's disability plan that make you uncomfortable, buy your own policy to either supplement or replace that plan.

TWO DISABILITY PLANS

Even if you have disability insurance, it may not start for several months after the paychecks stop, or it may cover only a portion of your expenses. To help you identify where you can get needed cash during that time, we've provided two worksheets: an *Emergency Disability Plan* (#45) to tide you over the first ninety days, and a *Long-Term Disability Plan* (#46) for your long-range financial needs. After studying the two plans (below), complete these two worksheets, and you'll have a sound emergency financial strategy you can activate if necessary. You may never need to use it, but you'll be comforted to know you're prepared.

An Emergency Disability Plan

This plan identifies three important areas: sources of ready cash, expenses, and emergency plans of action.

Ready cash. This comes from primary sources, which is money already available, and secondary sources, which are funds you need to apply for. (You may find the information in Chapter 5, Borrowing, helpful.)

If you don't have disability insurance, or if you have any problem with your disability coverage, look over the many sources of possible funds listed on the worksheet to see what you may have available. Discuss each source with your spouse.

For example, you may have a valuable collection you can convert to ready cash. A friend of ours, for instance, has race horses and guns. Because his wife, Priscilla, doesn't understand much about either, Jock prepared an emergency liquidation plan. "Jock wrote a list of which horses to sell first and where to sell them," Priscilla said. "Then he labeled his guns, and told me which to keep for their antique value and where to take the rest for consignment."

Expenses. These can only be estimated, but your budgeting worksheets (#s 23–27) will be helpful. Review them with a disabled family member in mind. Some expenses, like medical costs, will increase; others will decrease. If the patient is not at a local hospital, you'll have the additional costs of transportation, extra child care, or food for friends or relatives. Even if your spouse is home, you may have to pay for chores that he or she did, like mowing the lawn or cleaning the house. Try to project what new costs you'll incur and add them to your regular expenses to get a realistic picture of your cash needs.

We realize there's no way to estimate accurately what your expenses might total. Just being aware they may occur is one reason for keeping close tabs on possible sources of cash.

Emergency plans of action. Start with a review of your budget to see what expenses you can reduce or eliminate during this period. Knowing where you can cut costs is one key to managing during a disability; the other is the creation of immediate cash to cover necessary expenses.

Then list all your creditors whom you think might defer payment, or accept an extended payment period. Many creditors will be willing to accommodate you in special circumstances. No creditor wants to see you trapped financially and unable to pay at all. A sound creditor plan will stretch your dollars.

Notify the insurance company that issued the disability policy and recheck your medical insurance for exact coverage and deductibles. Then mobilize your support networks. We've listed some of these in the worksheet to give you an idea of the kind of action plan you can create, and to trigger your own thoughts. Assess your individual situation to see where you can turn for help and support.

Review your emergency plans periodically, and when your sources of ready cash or your expenses change dramatically, update the plan.

A Long-Term Disability Plan

This plan focuses on long-range solutions. It formalizes the temporary budget cuts of the three-month emergency period so you can put together a workable financial guide for the long haul.

On the *Long-Term Disability Plan* (#46) worksheet list your monthly disability insurance income. Then list any funds still remaining from your ninety-day emergency plan and any other continuing source of funds. Compare this total with your estimated expenses to determine how much, if any, you must reduce your expenses.

Now tackle a prearranged expense reduction plan. Using your regular budget worksheets (#s 23–27), decide what expenses you can reduce permanently, and by how much.

If you or your spouse are disabled, after the first three months you may have an idea of how long the disability will last, and how you'll need to budget your funds. With your austerity income and expenses clearly documented, you'll be able to determine if your income covers your expenses and, if not, what the deficit will be.

At the time, you'll want to develop alternative sources of income to meet any shortfall. You'll want to consider full-time and part-time work, and if you have young children, establishing a business at home.

You may also have other income-producing resources: an extra bedroom to rent out, or a teenage child who can contribute to the family kitty by shoveling snow, baby-sitting, washing cars, or mowing lawns. Grace W. Weinstein, author of *The Lifetime Book of Money Management*, says, "Look to the earnings of other family members. Now, if ever, is the time for you all to pull together."

As always with managing your money, if your expenses and sources of income change significantly, draw up a revised version of this long-term plan.

WHEN A DEATH
OCCURS

14

"As I was driving to the hospital, I didn't really want to think about what I felt—I felt he wasn't going to be all right at all," said Carol. "And when the doctor came into the waiting room, I knew. The paramedics had never gotten a heartbeat on him."

Carol, a young Chicago mother, has relived that day many times since Bud's fatal heart attack in his office. It is a memory laced with many emotions—disbelief, shock, grief, even irony. Just the evening before, they had taken their twelve-year-old daughter shopping for her coming birthday.

"We sat in the mall and watched her, and talked about how great she was and what a joy it was to see her grow." Even after two years, it's still hard for Carol to talk about that day. "It was terrible," she says softly. "Words can't describe it."

Carol was caught totally off guard by the call from Bud's secretary, but even if you have warning, is a wife ever prepared for the shock of her husband's death? Sally is a woman in New York whose husband had Hodgkin's disease for ten years. "It went on for so long that I began to think everything would be all right," she said, "and then Peter's health started to fail and it was touch and go for the last two years. When he finally died, I couldn't believe it."

You can expect a seriously ill person to die, yet still not anticipate the shock of that loss. An unexpected death, like Bud's, simply stuns the mind and body. You're unprepared to deal with it either emotionally or logically.

Emotional recovery takes hard work and time. But unfortunately, the legal and financial demands of a death don't leave us enough time to regain a clear-thinking mind or a logical perspective. Just at this moment of crisis you—the survivor—must make dozens of difficult, critical decisions about your family's business and future.

Because too many mistakes are made during this traumatic period, you'll find a *Transition Plan Checklist* (#47) in the Workbook section of this book to guide you through the first difficult months. We have expanded a chronology in *The Widow's Guide to Life*, by Ida Fisher and Byron Lane, (Lane Con Press, 1985) to provide a checklist of the various details you should discharge after a death, many of them legally required. By lifting the burden of finding out what to do, this checklist allows you to act almost automatically.

Carol remembered the first days after Bud died. "I was numb and in a state of shock, which I guess was fortunate. You can function fine in shock. I would just concentrate on whatever I had to do." With the *Transition Plan Checklist* (#47) in hand, you'll know exactly what you have to do, and when.

You'll also learn what you don't have to do. "You'll be besieged with advice from relatives, friends, and your husband's associates," said Julie, the family counselor who has been a widow for seven years. "You know: move out of your house right away; sell the second car; talk to my wonderful money manager who can invest your life insurance money." When you know what must be done, you'll also know what can be deferred. Understanding that there are decisions you can postpone can relieve some of the stress, because all the people we met—widows, widowers, and divorcées—agreed that the worst time to make a decision is right after a traumatic event.

As you review the Transition Plan below, you'll see there are many tedious tasks. Don't be discouraged. They do take time. You may want to follow Carol's example. "Even with the good accountants, attorneys, and other people who helped me, it took a lot of time to collect information and get the right documents to the right people," she said. "I decided to take one year off and get all the paperwork done, before finding a job."

THE TRANSITION PLAN

Whether you track down the information and file the necessary papers yourself, or you delegate tasks to other people, make it your responsibility to keep the *Transition Plan Checklist* (#47) up to date. It's your best way of being sure that important documents are filed and decisions are made within the necessary time.

As you can see from the chronology, some decisions must be made at once, others can wait for six to nine months or longer. Within each time period, they are listed in order of decreasing urgency.

At Once

1. Make funeral arrangements. If you are one of the few couples who have already made funeral plans, you'll be grateful for that guidance. Most people are like Sally. "There was a lot of planning in those last months of Peter's illness," she said, "but the one thing I could never bring myself to discuss was the funeral. Peter tried to talk about it once. 'Don't waste money on a funeral,' he said. In the end, I muddled through by myself."

2. Decide on obituary notices. You may not want to notify your local newspapers if you have small children or a large estate, and particularly if your spouse's death is not unexpected; you will avoid calls from salesmen and other people at a difficult time. However, you may want to send a notice to former hometown papers, school alumni associations, and other professional organizations.

3. Notify relatives.

4. Notify friends or, better yet, ask close friends to help you with this difficult task.

5. Open a checking account in your own name, if you don't already have one.

Within the First 30 Days

1. Get at least twenty *certified* copies of the death certificate. You'll need to produce them for many reasons, such as collecting life insurance claims, transferring title or ownership of properties, cars, etc. In most cases, the funeral home can get the copies for your.

2. Put all joint checking and savings accounts in your name, and keep those accounts separate from any probate proceedings. Your bank will probably request that you maintain a reserve in the old account for any checks that may be outstanding.

3. Establish a new "estate" bank account in the name of the deceased for the checks that will come in, such as life insurance proceeds. The funds can probably not be used until probate is completed, but at least they will draw interest in a safe account. After probate, these funds will pay the estate's bills.

4. Notify all insurance companies, and start to file for benefits.

5. Review the auto insurance policy. It may carry medical or accidental death and dismemberment coverage in addition to the life insurance benefits.

6. Check your medical insurance policies immediately for any time limitations for filing claims for benefits. Also check the benefits themselves to see if additional coverage, such as accidental death, can be claimed. Ask your insurance agent to do this for you.

7. If the death was accidental and occurred while traveling, notify all the credit card companies; many of them automatically include travel accident insurance as part of their services.

8. Report the death to the local Social Security Administration office, and ask them to send you its guide on Social Security benefits. Social Security benefits are not automatic.

9. Apply for Social Security benefits. You must appear personally with the following documents in hand: a copy of the death certificate, a copy of your marriage certificate, both your Social Security numbers, a copy of your birth certificate, copies of birth certificates of all children under age eighteen (even if they are from former marriages), and verification of your spouse's earnings (you can use the last income tax return).

10. If your spouse was a veteran, contact the Veteran's Administration

for benefits. Some states have their own veteran's benefits. Both the federal and state governments will want the same information you furnished the Social Security Administration, plus a copy of the discharge papers. If you can't locate them, write to the National Personnel Records Center, Military Personnel Records, 9700 Page Boulevard, St. Louis, MO 63132.

11. Notify your spouse's employer or associates, but don't assume they will automatically file for the benefits that are due you. Make a friend of someone in the office to help you; normally the personnel department has someone skilled in this area.

12. If the death was work-related, file for Workers Compensation benefits. You would make a claim through your spouse's employer, who would file it with its Workers Compensation insurance company.

13. Check all places where your spouse might have purchased life insurance: clubs, fraternal, professional, or charitable organizations, school alumni associations, credit life insurance on loans, or travel life insurance through credit cards.

14. Have your broker transfer all securities to your name as soon as possible. By transferring title, you will acquire a source of ready cash, if needed. If your securities were held in joint tenancy, they will not have to go through probate.

15. If you have U.S. Savings Bonds in joint tenancy, you can either have the bank reissue them in your name or cash them in at once. They won't have to go through probate.

16. Your safe-deposit box, which in most states is sealed after a death, can be opened under certain circumstances. If you furnish a certified copy of the death certificate, you can look for a will, burial instructions, or life insurance policies.

If some of the contents of the box are your separate property, you have the right to remove them so they are not included in the estate. The bank may require proof of your ownership, such as a bill of sale.

Get another safe-deposit box so you can protect your valuables in the interim while the family box is sealed, which will be until probate is completed.

17. Notify all IRA and Keogh accounts. The manner in which the account was set up will determine how its funds are distributed.

18. If you are short of funds, refer to Chapter 5, Borrowing, and the *Emergency Disability Plan* (#45) for ways to find ready cash.

19. Look for assets in the income tax records. For example, Schedule B lists interest and dividend income, and names each stock, mutual fund, and taxable bond that generated income. If you don't have a copy of the return, get one from your accountant or regional office of the Internal Revenue Service.

Within the Next 60 Days

1. Select an estate attorney to represent your interests and to file the will. Your regular attorney may not specialize in estates, and he may have

a conflict of interest if he also represents your spouse's business. See Chapter 2, Picking Your Advisory Team, for help in finding an attorney.

2. Pick an accountant to handle the financial transactions that will occur during this period. He must file federal estate and inheritance tax returns. Work closely with him on those transactions. Again, your spouse's accountant may have a conflict of interest that will force you to select a new advisor.

3. Transfer title on your home and any other real estate that you owned jointly to your own name.

4. Transfer title on the cars. The way in which title was jointly held and how the estate is being settled will govern how the transfer may be made. If the bank holds title to your car, the bank's loan officer will help you with the transfer.

5. Notify your insurance agent to change the auto and homeowner's policies to your name.

6. Cancel and change all credit cards to your name. To protect your credit, make sure you pay all bills promptly. If you don't feel ready for that yet, ask your accountant to pay them for you for a time.

7. Change all the utilities to your name.

8. Change the listing in the telephone directory; for personal security women should use only their first initial, not their first name.

9. If your spouse was a beneficiary on your life insurance policies, notify your life insurance agent to remove his or her name.

10. Review your own medical insurance to be sure it is adequate.

11. Revise your will to reflect your current situation and desires.

12. Notify all creditors of your situation.

13. Select a financial advisor to counsel you on your investments (you may be receiving large sums of money from life insurance benefits), but try to postpone any major decisions you don't feel up to making and be conservative in those you do. If possible, pick an advisor who only counsels, not sells.

Within the Next 6 Months

1. Work up a new budget for the means you now have on hand. Use the worksheets in Chapter 7, Budgeting.

2. Review your life insurance needs to be sure you are including all the beneficiaries you want to, and that you are protecting the estate adequately.

3. Update your will.

4. Since you will have revised much of your financial information following the death, record this new financial data on appropriate worksheets in the Workbook section so it's up to date for your heirs if anything happens to you. Review all the worksheets in light of your new status, especially #s 1 to 11, which are explained in Chapter 1, Keeping Family Records and Documents.

5. Review the *Disability Insurance Checklist* (#44) to see if you are adequately protected.

6. Consult with your financial advisor about starting your investment plan so that all your assets are protected.

7. Take time to review all your records going back at least two years— check stubs, bank statements, and business correspondence—to search for additional life insurance coverage and other assets you didn't know existed.

8. Review the *Checklist of Executor's Duties* (#48) and make certain the executor is doing his job.

WORKBOOK

WORKSHEETS AND CHECKLISTS

This workbook is perforated so you have the choice of working in the book or detaching the pages. If you need additional copies of any page—for updating your information, for correcting errors, for your own note taking, or just to have a complete set on hand (and that's a good idea)—you can duplicate the pages right from the book, or remove them first, if you prefer.

#18   Interview Questions for Financial Institutions
#19   Financial Institution Evaluation Guide
#20   Collateral Guarantee or Co-Signature Record
#21   Loan Interest Rate Comparison
#22   Emergency Cash Plan
#23   Daily Cash Budgeting Worksheet
#24   Monthly Expense Budgeting Worksheet
#25   Annual Expense Budgeting Worksheet
#26   Discretionary Expense Worksheet
#27   Monthly Budget Control Worksheet
#28   List of Ownership of Assets
#29   Estate Planning Checklist
#30   Will Preparation Worksheet
#31   When to Review a Will
#32   Evaluation Guide: Individual Executor or Trustee
#33   Evaluation Guide: Institutional Executor or Trustee
#34   Evaluation Guide: Guardian of the Person
#35   Evaluation Guide: Guardian of the Estate
#36   Trustee Evaluation Guide
#37   Childproof Protection Summary
#38   Life Insurance Worksheet
#39   Dependent Income Worksheet
#40   Beneficiary Worksheet
#41   Medical Insurance Coverage Worksheet
#42   Medical Insurance Cost/Coverage Comparison
#43   Evaluating HMO and Group Insurance
#44   Disability Insurance Checklist
#45   Emergency Disability Plan
#46   Long-Term Disability Plan
#47   Transition Plan Checklist
       At Once
       Within the First 30 Days
       Within the Next 60 Days
       Within the Next 6 Months
#48   Checklist of Executor's Duties

LOCATION OF IMPORTANT PAPERS

Completed as of _____

Type of Document	Location				Length of Time to Keep
	Home File	Safe-Deposit Box	Office	Other	
1. PERSONAL					
Certificate of birth	[ ]	[ ]	[ ]	[ ]	Permanently
Certificate of marriage	[ ]	[ ]	[ ]	[ ]	Permanently
Certificate of divorce	[ ]	[ ]	[ ]	[ ]	Permanently
Social Security cards	[ ]	[ ]	[ ]	[ ]	Permanently
Military discharge	[ ]	[ ]	[ ]	[ ]	Permanently
Passports	[ ]	[ ]	[ ]	[ ]	Permanently
Wills	[ ]	[ ]	[ ]	[ ]	Permanently
Death certificate	[ ]	[ ]	[ ]	[ ]	Permanently
2. FINANCIAL					
Bank account information	[ ]	[ ]	[ ]	[ ]	7 years
Loan agreements	[ ]	[ ]	[ ]	[ ]	While in force

LOCATION OF IMPORTANT PAPERS (Cont.)

Completed as of _____

Type of Document	Home File	Safe-Deposit Box	Office	Other	Length of Time to Keep
Stocks and bonds	[ ]	[ ]	[ ]	[ ]	Permanently
Government securities	[ ]	[ ]	[ ]	[ ]	Permanently
Notes due to others or you	[ ]	[ ]	[ ]	[ ]	Length of note
Passbooks	[ ]	[ ]	[ ]	[ ]	While in force
Pension or profit-sharing plan information	[ ]	[ ]	[ ]	[ ]	Permanently
IRA and Keogh plan	[ ]	[ ]	[ ]	[ ]	Permanently
Other items _____	[ ]	[ ]	[ ]	[ ]	_____
_____	[ ]	[ ]	[ ]	[ ]	_____
_____	[ ]	[ ]	[ ]	[ ]	_____
3. TAXES					
Past returns	[ ]	[ ]	[ ]	[ ]	7 years
Canceled checks	[ ]	[ ]	[ ]	[ ]	7 years

Location

Other _____

_____

4. INSURANCE

Life insurance policies	[ ] [ ] [ ] [ ]	Permanently
Homeowners policy	[ ] [ ] [ ] [ ]	1 year
Auto policy	[ ] [ ] [ ] [ ]	1 year
Major Medical	[ ] [ ] [ ] [ ]	1 year
Other _____	[ ] [ ] [ ] [ ]	
_____		

5. REAL ESTATE

Trust deeds	[ ] [ ] [ ] [ ]	Permanently
Real estate notes	[ ] [ ] [ ] [ ]	Permanently
Title policy	[ ] [ ] [ ] [ ]	Permanently
Mortgage documents	[ ] [ ] [ ] [ ]	Permanently
Tax assessments	[ ] [ ] [ ] [ ]	7 years
Rental agreements	[ ] [ ] [ ] [ ]	3 years
Rental receipts	[ ] [ ] [ ] [ ]	3 years
Receipts for repairs	[ ] [ ] [ ] [ ]	3 years
Receipts for improvements	[ ] [ ] [ ] [ ]	Permanently

LOCATION OF IMPORTANT PAPERS (Cont.)

Completed as of _____

Type of Document	Location				Length of Time to Keep
	Home File	Safe-Deposit Box	Office	Other	
Other _____	[ ]	[ ]	[ ]	[ ]	_____
_____	[ ]	[ ]	[ ]	[ ]	_____
6. MEDICAL					
Records	[ ]	[ ]	[ ]	[ ]	Permanently
Receipts	[ ]	[ ]	[ ]	[ ]	1 year
Insurance payments	[ ]	[ ]	[ ]	[ ]	1 year
7. AUTOS					
Registration	[ ]	[ ]	[ ]	[ ]	Until sold
Ownership	[ ]	[ ]	[ ]	[ ]	Until sold
Loan agreement	[ ]	[ ]	[ ]	[ ]	3 years
Loan payment records	[ ]	[ ]	[ ]	[ ]	1 year
Lease agreement	[ ]	[ ]	[ ]	[ ]	Length of lease
Repair records	[ ]	[ ]	[ ]	[ ]	3 years

8. SAFE-DEPOSIT BOX INFO

Permanently   [ ]   [ ]   [ ]   [ ]

_____

_____

_____

Persons authorized:

_____

_____

_____

9. POWER OF ATTORNEY

Names

Permanently   [ ]   [ ]   [ ]   [ ]

_____

_____

_____

10. MISCELLANEOUS ITEMS

A Family Survival Kit

Permanently   [ ]   [ ]   [ ]   [ ]   _____

[ ]   [ ]   [ ]   [ ]   _____

[ ]   [ ]   [ ]   [ ]   _____

[ ]   [ ]   [ ]   [ ]   _____

LOCATION OF IMPORTANT PAPERS (Cont.)

Completed as of _____

Type of Document	Location				Length of Time to Keep
	Home File	Safe-Deposit Box	Office	Other	
_____	☐	☐	☐	☐	_____
_____	☐	☐	☐	☐	_____
_____	☐	☐	☐	☐	_____
_____	☐	☐	☐	☐	_____
_____	☐	☐	☐	☐	_____

Special remarks: _____

_____

_____

_____

For more information, see page 5.

BANKING INFORMATION

Completed as of _____

Name of Bank	Account No.	Branch	Address	Bank Contact	Type of Account: Joint (J), Husband (H), Wife (W), Trust (T)	Checking (C), Savings (S), Money Market (M)

For more information, see page 7.

LIST OF STOCK SECURITIES
As of _____

Name of Security	No. of Shares	Owner	Type	Original Cost	Current Value per Share	Total Current Value
				$	$	$

For more information, see page 7.

LIST OF BOND SECURITIES
As of _____

Type	Owner	Interest Rate	Due Date	$
				$
				$

For more information, see page 7.

CURRENT INSURANCE POLICIES

For the year

_____

Insurance for:	Insuring Company	Policy No.	Expiration Date
Automobiles (Liability, Fire, Theft, Collision)	_____	_____	_____
Residence Building	_____	_____	_____
Contents	_____	_____	_____
Second Home	_____	_____	_____
Liability to Others (Non-auto)	_____	_____	_____
Extra Liability Limits (Personal Umbrella)	_____	_____	_____
Medical and Surgical	_____	_____	_____
Major Medical	_____	_____	_____
Excess Major Medical	_____	_____	_____
Life Insurance	_____	_____	_____
	_____	_____	_____
	_____	_____	_____
	_____	_____	_____
	_____	_____	_____
Disability	_____	_____	_____
Other	_____	_____	_____

For more information, see page 7.

REAL ESTATE PROPERTIES

As of _____

Property Address	Description 1. Home 2. Vacation Home 3. Commercial 4. Industrial 5. Residential Investment	Approxi- mate Value	Holder of Loan
1.			
2.			
3.			
4.			
5.			

REAL ESTATE PROPERTIES (Cont.)

As of _____

Property Address	Description 1. Home 2. Vacation Home 3. Commercial 4. Industrial 5. Residential Investment	Approxi-mate Value	Holder of Loan
6. _____	_____	_____	_____
7. _____	_____	_____	_____
8. _____	_____	_____	_____

For more information, see page 8.

SAFE-DEPOSIT BOX INFORMATION AND CONTENTS

Compiled as of

_____

Location of Box: _____

_____

Key No.: _____

Locations of Keys: _____

_____

_____

Persons Authorized to Enter the Box:

_____

_____

_____

_____

Contents of Box: _____

_____

_____

_____

_____

_____

_____

_____

_____

_____

For more information, see page 8.

FAMILY STATUS RECORD

As of _____

Husband's Name: RUSTY AURE MALIGAYA

Date of Birth: 9-8-58   Soc. Sec. # _____

Wife's Name: MONICA DEL ROSARIO MALIGAYA

Date of Birth: 3-24-61   Soc. Sec. # 557-57-5066

Home Address: 298 DENNIS DRIVE DALY CITY CA 94015

Business Address: (H) 415 878-5853

(W) 415 777-8951

Children's Names and Addresses	Sex	Date of Birth	Married, Divorced, or Single	Soc. Sec. #
JUSTINE RAQUEL MALIGAYA	F	4-12-85	S	

FAMILY STATUS RECORD (Cont.)

As of

_____

Grandchildren's Names and Addresses	Sex	Date of Birth	Married, Divorced, or Single	Soc. Sec. #
_____	___	_____	_____	_____
_____	___	_____	_____	_____
_____	___	_____	_____	_____
_____	___	_____	_____	_____
_____	___	_____	_____	_____
_____	___	_____	_____	_____
_____	___	_____	_____	_____
_____	___	_____	_____	_____
_____				
_____				

Others to Be Considered: Names and Addresses	Sex	Date of Birth	Relationship	Soc. Sec. #
_____	___	_____	_____	_____
_____				
_____	___	_____	_____	_____
_____	___	_____	_____	_____
_____	___	_____	_____	_____
_____	___	_____	_____	_____
_____	___	_____	_____	_____
_____				

For more information, see page 9.

NOTES
INFORMATION

NOTES DUE YOU

Person Owing	Amount	Due Date	Interest Rate
_____	_____	_____	_____
_____	_____	_____	_____
_____	_____	_____	_____

Additional information on notes: _____

_____

_____

NOTES DUE OTHERS

Owed to	Amount	Due Date	Interest Rate
_____	_____	_____	_____
_____	_____	_____	_____
_____	_____	_____	_____

Additional information on notes: _____

_____

_____

For more information, see page 9.

LIST OF
CREDIT CARDS
Compiled as of _____

Name of Card	Card #	Expiration Date	Authorized Card Users	Telephone Contact if Lost or Stolen

For more information, see page 10.

LIST OF IMPORTANT ADVISORS

As of

_____

Personal Attorney: _____

Name of Firm: _____

Address: _____

Telephone (Bus.) _____ (Res.) _____

Business Attorney: _____

Name of Firm: _____

Address: _____

Telephone (Bus.) _____ (Res.) _____

Personal Accountant: _____

Name of Firm: _____

Address: _____

Telephone (Bus.) _____ (Res.) _____

Personal Banker: _____

Name of Bank: _____

Address: _____

Telephone (Bus.) _____ (Res.) _____

Life Insurance Agent: _____

Name of Firm: _____

Address: _____

Telephone (Bus.) _____ (Res.) _____

LIST OF IMPORTANT ADVISORS (Cont.)

As of

_____

Automobile Agent: _____

Name of Firm: _____

Address: _____

Telephone (Bus.) _____ (Res.) _____

Homeowner's Insurance Agent: _____

Name of Firm: _____

Address: _____

Telephone (Bus.) _____ (Res.) _____

Investment Advisor: _____

Name of Firm: _____

Address: _____

Telephone (Bus.) _____ (Res.) _____

Doctor's Name: _____

Address: _____

Telephone (Bus.) _____ (Res.) _____

Specialty: _____

Doctor's Name: _____

Address: _____

Telephone (Bus.) _____ (Res.) _____

Specialty: _____

**LIST OF
IMPORTANT
ADVISORS**
(Cont.)

As of

_____

Doctor's Name: _____

Address: _____

Telephone (Bus.) _____ *(Res.)* _____

Specialty: _____

Dentist's Name: _____

Address: _____

Telephone (Bus.) _____ *(Res.)* _____

For more information,
see page 13.

INTERVIEW QUESTIONS FOR PROSPECTIVE ADVISORS

1. *What is their specialty?*

   _____

   _____

2. *What kind of clientele do they represent?*

   _____

   _____

3. *What is their educational background?*

   _____

   _____

4. *Have they achieved any professional designations in their field?*

   _____

   _____

5. *How long have they practiced in this field?*

   _____

   _____

6. *How long have they been with this particular firm?*

   _____

   _____

7. *What professional associations do they belong to?*

   _____

   _____

8. *How large is their organization?*

   _____

   _____

INTERVIEW QUESTIONS FOR PROSPECTIVE ADVISORS (Cont.)

9. *Will they be the people who would deal with you?*

_____

_____

10. *What is the fee structure?*

_____

_____

11. *Who takes over if advisor is unavailable, out of town, or ill?*

_____

_____

12. *Will it be easy to speak to advisor when I call?*

_____

_____

13. *Would they give a home telephone number and can they be contacted there with a problem?*

_____

_____

14. _____

_____

_____

15. _____

_____

_____

16. _____

_____

_____

For more information, see page 13.

ADVISOR
EVALUATION
GUIDE

Name of Potential Advisor: _____

Date of Interview: _____

Rating System: 1 (unsatisfactory) to 10 (excellent)

Evaluation Areas	Rating
Quality of area where office is located	_____
Educational background of advisor	_____
Work experience as it applies to my problem	_____
Size of organization	_____
Fee structure	_____
Ability to relate to me	_____
Accessibility	_____
Appearance of office	_____
Attitude of receptionist	_____
Convenience of office location	_____

TOTAL: _____

Strong points: _____

_____

Weak points: _____

_____

Additional comments: _____

_____

For more information, see page 13.

RECORD OF ASSETS

As of

Cash

Money on hand $ _____

Balance in checking account   _____   _____

Balance in savings account   _____

Securities

Money market funds $ _____

Stock market investments   _____

Bonds   _____

U.S. Savings Bonds   _____

Mutual funds   _____

Other investments (CDs, government securities, or
repurchase agreements)   _____

Cash Surrender Value of Life Insurance Policies $ _____

Notes Receivable $ _____

Real Estate $ _____

Autos and Other Vehicles $ _____

Pension and/or Profit-Sharing Funds $ _____

Individual Retirement and Keogh Accounts $ _____

Other Assets

Home furnishings and household goods $ _____

Jewelry, furs, and silver   _____

Art and antiques   _____

Other personal property   _____

RECORD
OF ASSETS
(Cont.)

As of

_____

Other items _____ _____

_____ _____

_____ _____

TOTAL ASSETS $ _____

For more information,
see page 22.

RECORD OF LIABILITIES

As of _____

Accounts Payable
Charge cards $ _____

Credit cards   _____

Medical bills and utilities   _____

Alimony and child support   _____

Other _____   _____

_____   _____

Contracts Payable
Automobiles $ _____

Furniture   _____

Installment credit contracts   _____

Notes Payable to Others
Banks $ _____

Real estate mortgages   _____

Others _____   _____

Taxes
Property taxes $ _____

Federal taxes   _____

State taxes   _____

TOTAL LIABILITIES $ _____

RECORD OF LIABILITIES (Cont.)

As of
_____

Total of Net Worth, as of _____ $ _____

Assets   _____

Liabilities   – _____

Net worth   = _____

To check your figures, make sure your assets equal your liabilities plus your net worth.

For more information,
see page 22.

BANKING SERVICES CHECKLIST

Services	Services Wanted	(NAME) Will Provide	(NAME) Will Provide
1. Checking Accounts			
Regular	[ ]	[ ]	[ ]
Bank by mail	[ ]	[ ]	[ ]
Drive-in teller service	[ ]	[ ]	[ ]
Check guarantee card	[ ]	[ ]	[ ]
Overdraft protection Limit: _____	[ ]	[ ]	[ ]
Market rate account	[ ]	[ ]	[ ]
Money market mutual fund	[ ]	[ ]	[ ]
2. Savings Accounts			
Passbook	[ ]	[ ]	[ ]
Trust	[ ]	[ ]	[ ]
Custodial	[ ]	[ ]	[ ]
Certificates of Deposit	[ ]	[ ]	[ ]
3. Bank Credit Card Limit: _____	[ ]	[ ]	[ ]
4. Undisbursed Loan Limit: _____	[ ]	[ ]	[ ]
5. Investment Counseling	[ ]	[ ]	[ ]
6. Trust Services	[ ]	[ ]	[ ]
7. Saturday Banking	[ ]	[ ]	[ ]
8. Banking Hours	[ ]	[ ]	[ ]
9. Loans			
Personal	[ ]	[ ]	[ ]
Home improvement	[ ]	[ ]	[ ]
Auto	[ ]	[ ]	[ ]

BANKING SERVICES CHECKLIST (Cont.)

	Education	[ ]	[ ]	[ ]
	Other _____	[ ]	[ ]	[ ]
10.	Safe-Deposit Box	[ ]	[ ]	[ ]
11.	Keogh Plan	[ ]	[ ]	[ ]
12.	Individual Retirement Accounts	[ ]	[ ]	[ ]

For more information,
see page 28.

PREPARATION CHECKLIST FOR MEETING WITH A FINANCIAL INSTITUTION

Name of institution: _____

Meeting date: _____

Target date for completion of items: _____

Item	Source of Information	Check If to Be Included	Check When Item Completed
Copy of Income Tax Returns			
19_____	_____	[ ]	[ ]
19_____	_____	[ ]	[ ]
19_____	_____	[ ]	[ ]
Financial Statement	_____	[ ]	[ ]
Budget Estimates	_____	[ ]	[ ]
Copy of Will	_____	[ ]	[ ]
Copy of Trust Agreement	_____	[ ]	[ ]
List of All Real Property	_____	[ ]	[ ]
Other	_____	[ ]	[ ]
	_____	[ ]	[ ]
	_____	[ ]	[ ]

For more information, see page 28.

INTERVIEW QUESTIONS FOR FINANCIAL INSTITUTIONS

Name:

_____

1. *How long have you been in business?*

_____

_____

2. *What are your gross assets?*

_____

_____

3. *What is the percentage of your deposits to your assets?*

_____

_____

4. *Where is your home office located?*

_____

_____

5. *How many branch offices do you have?*

_____

_____

6. *Who would be in charge of my account?*

_____

_____

7. *How long has this person worked in this office?*

_____

_____

INTERVIEW QUESTIONS FOR FINANCIAL INSTITUTIONS

Name:

_____

8. *What is that person's title?*

_____

_____

9. *What is that person's financial background?*

_____

_____

10. *What are your bank service charges or penalties?*

_____

_____

For more information,
see page 28.

FINANCIAL
INSTITUTION
EVALUATION
GUIDE

Name of institution: _____

Person interviewed: _____ Date _____

Rating system: 1 (unsatisfactory) to 10 (excellent)

Evaluation Areas	Rating
Appearance of branch	_____
Safety of area where located	_____
Attitude of employees	_____
Convenience of location	_____
Convenience of operating hours	_____
Reputation in the community	_____
Services available	_____
Financial stability	_____
TOTAL	_____

Strong points: _____

_____

Weak points: _____

_____

Additional comments: _____

_____

For more information,
see page 28.

COLLATERAL GUARANTEE OR CO-SIGNATURE RECORD

Effective Date	Person or Institution	Amount Involved	Type of Collateral	Due Date

For more information, see page 35.

LOAN INTEREST RATE COMPARISON

Institution   Rate of Interest

Banks	Over-draft	Bank Card	Auto	Mortgage	Personal
_____	_____	_____	_____	_____	_____
_____	_____	_____	_____	_____	_____
_____	_____	_____	_____	_____	_____
_____	_____	_____	_____	_____	_____

Savings and Loans	Over-draft	Bank Card	Auto	Mortgage	Personal
_____	_____	_____	_____	_____	_____
_____	_____	_____	_____	_____	_____
_____	_____	_____	_____	_____	_____
_____	_____	_____	_____	_____	_____

Other	Over-draft	Bank Card	Auto	Mortgage	Personal
_____	_____	_____	_____	_____	_____
_____	_____	_____	_____	_____	_____
_____	_____	_____	_____	_____	_____
_____	_____	_____	_____	_____	_____

For more information,
see page 37.

EMERGENCY CASH PLAN

Plan arranged as of

_____

Estimated Amounts
_____

Primary Sources of Ready Cash

Extra reserve maintained in checking account $ _____

Overdraft limit in checking account   _____

Savings account   _____

Money market funds   _____

Cashable securities (stocks and bonds)   _____

Credit card limits   _____

Prearranged undisbursed loan   _____

Total ready cash from primary sources: $ _____

Secondary Sources of Immediate Cash

Borrow on cash value of life insurance policies $ _____

Borrow from credit union   _____

Borrow from profit-sharing plan   _____

Borrow from personal loan companies   _____

Secure loan on car or increase present loan   _____

Sell second car   _____

Take out second or third mortgage on home   _____

Change income tax withholding   _____

Pawn jewelry   _____

Borrow from friends and/or relatives   _____

EMERGENCY
CASH PLAN
(Cont.)

**Estimated
Amounts**

Plan arranged as of

_____

Secondary Sources of Immediate Cash

Secure loan from employer _____

Emergency cash in Keogh or IRA accounts _____

Total ready cash from secondary sources: $ _____

Total potential cash from all sources: $ _____

For more information,
see page 37.

DAILY CASH BUDGETING WORKSHEET

For the week of _____

Item	Monday	Tuesday	Wednesday	Thursday	Friday	Saturday	Sunday
Groceries							
Meals eaten out							
Clothing purchases							
Laundry and dry cleaning							
Entertainment (movies, plays, sporting events, toys, gifts, other)							
Health club							
Hairdresser							
Cosmetics and sundries							
Gas and oil							
Auto repairs (maintenance)							
Parking and tolls							
Public transportation							

DAILY CASH BUDGETING WORKSHEET (Cont.)

For the week of _____

	Monday	Tuesday	Wednesday	Thursday	Friday	Saturday	Sunday
School lunches							
Children's allowances							
Other _____							
TOTAL	$	$	$	$	$	$	$

For more information, see page 51.

MONTHLY EXPENSE BUDGETING WORKSHEET

Month of _____

List of Actual Expenses as They Occur

Item	Week 1	Week 2	Week 3	Week 4	Total Monthly Amount Spent
Housing					
Rent, condo, or mortgage payment					
Vacation home/rental property					
Property taxes					
Miscellaneous repairs					
Housekeeper					
				SUBTOTAL	$
Utilities and Home Expenses					
Gas					
Electricity					
Other fuel					
Telephone					
Water and sewer					
Cable T.V.					
Garbage collection					
Gardener					
Pool maintenance					
Pest control service					
				SUBTOTAL	$

MONTHLY EXPENSE BUDGETING WORKSHEET (Cont.)

Month of _____

List of Actual Expenses as They Occur

	Week 1	Week 2	Week 3	Week 4	Total Monthly Amount Spent
Personal Maintenance					
Groceries					
Meals eaten out					
Clothing purchases					
Laundry and dry cleaning					
Entertainment, including recreation and vacations					
Personal care, including health club, hairdresser, and cosmetics					
				SUBTOTAL	$
Transportation					
Gas and oil					
Repairs (maintenance)					
Parking and tolls					
License and registration					
Public transportation					
				SUBTOTAL	$

Insurance Premiums
Auto
Life
Health
Disability
Homeowners
_____
_____

SUBTOTAL $_____

Obligations
Installment contract payments
Furniture payments
Auto payments
Credit cards
Charge accounts
Dues and subscriptions
Taxes, federal
Taxes, state
Taxes, local

SUBTOTAL $_____

Child/Dependent Care
Baby-sitting fees
Nursery school fees
Special transportation
Lunches and miscellaneous items

SUBTOTAL $_____

Health Care
Dental visits
Doctors' visits
Drugs and vitamins

SUBTOTAL $_____

MONTHLY EXPENSE BUDGETING WORKSHEET (Cont.)

Month of _____

List of Actual Expenses as They Occur

Item	Week 1	Week 2	Week 3	Week 4	Total Monthly Amount Spent
Miscellaneous Expenses					
Spousal support					
Child support					
Education costs					
Retirement contributions					
Charitable contributions					
Legal fees					
Accountant fees					
Children's allowances					
Savings					
SUBTOTAL					$ _____
TOTAL ESTIMATED MONTHLY EXPENSES					$ _____

Completed as of _____

For more information, see page 51.

ANNUAL EXPENSE BUDGETING WORKSHEET

Item	Things I Must Have	Things I Don't Need	Annual Cost	Budgeted Avg. Monthly Amount	Actual Amount Spent
Housing					
Rent, condo, or mortgage payment	[ ]	[ ]	____	____	____
Vacation home/rental property	[ ]	[ ]	____	____	____
Property taxes	[ ]	[ ]	____	____	____
Miscellaneous repairs	[ ]	[ ]	____	____	____
Housekeeper	[ ]	[ ]	____	____	____
SUBTOTAL			$ ____	$ ____	$ ____
Utilities and Home Expenses					
Gas	[ ]	[ ]	____	____	____
Electricity	[ ]	[ ]	____	____	____
Other fuel	[ ]	[ ]	____	____	____
Telephone	[ ]	[ ]	____	____	____
Water and sewer	[ ]	[ ]	____	____	____
Cable T.V.	[ ]	[ ]	____	____	____

ANNUAL EXPENSE BUDGETING WORKSHEET (Cont.)

Item	Things I Must Have	Things I Don't Need	Annual Cost	Budgeted Avg. Monthly Amount	Actual Amount Spent
Housing					
Garbage collection	[ ]	[ ]			
Gardener	[ ]	[ ]			
Pool maintenance	[ ]	[ ]			
Pest control services	[ ]	[ ]			
SUBTOTAL			$	$	$
Personal Maintenance					
Groceries	[ ]	[ ]			
Meals eaten out	[ ]	[ ]			
Clothing purchases	[ ]	[ ]			
Laundry and dry cleaning	[ ]	[ ]			
Entertainment, including recreation and vacations	[ ]	[ ]			
Personal care, including health club, hairdresser, and cosmetics	[ ]	[ ]			
SUBTOTAL			$	$	$

Transportation

Gas and oil

Repairs (maintenance)

Parking and tolls

License and registration

Public transportation

SUBTOTAL $_____ $_____ $_____

Insurance Premiums

Auto

Life

Health

Disability

Homeowners

SUBTOTAL $_____ $_____ $_____

Obligations

Installment contract payments

Furniture payments

Auto payments

ANNUAL EXPENSE BUDGETING WORKSHEET (Cont.)

Item	Things I Must Have	Things I Don't Need	Annual Cost	Budgeted Avg. Monthly Amount	Actual Amount Spent
Housing					
Credit cards	[ ]	[ ]	___	___	___
Charge accounts	[ ]	[ ]	___	___	___
Dues and subscriptions	[ ]	[ ]	___	___	___
Taxes, federal	[ ]	[ ]	___	___	___
Taxes, state	[ ]	[ ]	___	___	___
Taxes, local	[ ]	[ ]	___	___	___
SUBTOTAL			$ ___	$ ___	$ ___
Child/Dependent Care					
Baby-sitting fees	[ ]	[ ]	___	___	___
Nursery school fees	[ ]	[ ]	___	___	___
Special transportation	[ ]	[ ]	___	___	___
Lunches and miscellaneous items	[ ]	[ ]	___	___	___
SUBTOTAL			$ ___	$ ___	$ ___

Health Care

Dental visits [ ] [ ] _____ _____

Doctors' visits [ ] [ ] _____ _____

Drugs and vitamins [ ] [ ] _____ _____

SUBTOTAL $ _____ $ _____ $ _____

Miscellaneous Expenses

Spousal support [ ] [ ] _____ _____

Child support [ ] [ ] _____ _____

Education costs [ ] [ ] _____ _____

Retirement contributions [ ] [ ] _____ _____

Charitable contributions [ ] [ ] _____ _____

Legal fees [ ] [ ] _____ _____

Accountant fees [ ] [ ] _____ _____

Children's allowances [ ] [ ] _____ _____

Savings [ ] [ ] _____ _____

SUBTOTAL $ _____

TOTAL ESTIMATED ANNUAL EXPENSES $ _____

Completed as of _____

For more information, see page 51.

DISCRETIONARY EXPENSE WORKSHEET

Items to be Eliminated	Monthly Amount Saved
_____	_____
_____	_____
_____	_____
_____	_____
_____	_____
_____	_____
_____	_____
_____	_____
_____	_____
_____	_____
_____	_____
_____	_____

TOTAL **$** _____

For more information,
see page 51.

MONTHLY BUDGET CONTROL WORKSHEET

Gross Monthly Income $ _____

Wages   _____

Salary   _____

Bonuses   _____

Real estate investments   _____

Dividends   _____

Interest   _____

Child support   _____

Alimony   _____

Other income   _____

_____   _____

_____   _____

_____   _____

TOTAL MONTHLY INCOME: _____

MONTHLY INCOME AND EXPENSE SUMMARY

Total Monthly Income: $ _____

Minus Total Monthly Expenses: – _____

Total monthly net discretionary income
    available: $ _____

Discretionary expenses eliminated: _____

**TOTAL MONTHLY
EXPENSE BUDGET:** $ _____

For more information,
see page 51.

LIST OF OWNERSHIP OF ASSETS
(Cont.)

As of _____

Item	Sole and Separate Property (H or W)	Type of Ownership		
		Joint Tenancy	Tenants in Common	Community Property
3. Bank _____	[ ]	[ ]	[ ]	[ ]
Acct. # _____				
Money Market Funds				
1. Name _____	[ ]	[ ]	[ ]	[ ]
Acct. # _____				
2. Name _____	[ ]	[ ]	[ ]	[ ]
Acct. # _____				
3. Name _____	[ ]	[ ]	[ ]	[ ]
Acct. # _____				

LIST OF OWNERSHIP OF ASSETS

As of _____

Type of Ownership

Item	Sole and Separate Property (H or W)	Joint Tenancy	Tenants in Common	Community Property
Savings				
1. Bank _____	[ ]	[ ]	[ ]	[ ]
Acct. # _____	[ ]	[ ]	[ ]	[ ]
2. Bank _____	[ ]	[ ]	[ ]	[ ]
Acct. # _____	[ ]	[ ]	[ ]	[ ]
3. Bank _____	[ ]	[ ]	[ ]	[ ]
Acct. # _____	[ ]	[ ]	[ ]	[ ]
4. Bank _____	[ ]	[ ]	[ ]	[ ]
Acct. # _____	[ ]	[ ]	[ ]	[ ]
Checking				
1. Bank _____	[ ]	[ ]	[ ]	[ ]
Acct. # _____	[ ]	[ ]	[ ]	[ ]
2. Bank _____				
Acct. # _____				

Stocks and Bonds

Mutual Funds

Autos and Other Vehicles

Pension Plans

LIST OF OWNERSHIP OF ASSETS
(Cont.)

As of _____

	Type of Ownership			
Item	Sole and Separate (H or W)	Joint	Tenants in Common	Community Property
IRAs and Keogh Plans				
1. Located _____	[ ]	[ ]	[ ]	[ ]
Acct. # _____				
2. Located _____	[ ]	[ ]	[ ]	[ ]
Acct. # _____				
Limited Partnerships				
_____	[ ]	[ ]	[ ]	[ ]
_____	[ ]	[ ]	[ ]	[ ]
Real Estate				
_____	[ ]	[ ]	[ ]	[ ]
_____	[ ]	[ ]	[ ]	[ ]

For more information, see page 56.

ESTATE PLANNING CHECKLIST

Item	Source of Information	Needed for Meeting	Target Date to Have Ready	Information Completed for Meeting
Income Tax Returns				
19___	_____	[ ]	____	[ ]
19___	_____	[ ]	____	[ ]
19___	_____	[ ]	____	[ ]
Financial Statement	(see Chap. 3)	[ ]	____	[ ]
List of Real Estate	(see Chap. 1)	[ ]	____	[ ]
Copy of Current Will	_____	[ ]	____	[ ]
Ownership of Assets Worksheet	(see Worksheet #28)	[ ]	____	[ ]
Life Insurance Policies	(see Chap. 1)	[ ]	____	[ ]
Will Preparation Worksheet	(see Chap. 9)	[ ]	____	[ ]

For more information, see page 56.

WILL PREPARATION WORKSHEET

Names of Beneficiaries
(Family, Friends, Charitable Institutions)

Relationship

Bequest
(Percentage of Estate, Cash Amount, or Article)

1. _____ _____ _____

2. _____ _____ _____

3. _____ _____ _____

4. _____ _____ _____

5. _____ _____ _____

6. _____ _____ _____

7. _____ _____ _____

8. _____ _____ _____

9. _____ _____ _____

10. _____ _____ _____

11. _____ _____ _____

12. _____ _____ _____

WILL PREPARATION WORKSHEET (Cont.)

Executor: *First Choice* _____

Successor _____

Trustee: *First Choice* _____

Successor or Alternate _____

For more information, see page 61.

WHEN TO REVIEW A WILL

	Check If Reviewed	Date

Family Relations
Separation or dissolution of marriage

Severe illness, death, incapacity, or death of a spouse

New grandchild

Economic and Personal Conditions
Significant financial gains or reversals

Acquisition of property in a different state

Change in life insurance insurability

Change in employment

Change in business interests: sale, purchase, incorporation, and/or dissolution of business

Change in health

Retirement

External Changes
Change in laws: state and federal income, estate, and gift tax laws; state property, trust, and probate laws

Change of residence to another state

Death, illness of the executor, trustee, guardian, or conservator to serve

For more information, see page 62.

EVALUATION GUIDE: INDIVIDUAL EXECUTOR OR TRUSTEE

Name of Nominee: _____

Review Date: _____

Rating System: 1 (unsatisfactory) to 10 (excellent)

Evaluation Areas	Rating
General business knowledge	_____
General knowledge of family situation	_____
Reputation	_____
Stability	_____
Maturity	_____
Time available	_____
Health	_____
Fiscal soundness	_____
Other _____	_____
_____	_____
_____	_____
TOTAL	_____

Strong points: _____

_____

Weak points: _____

_____

Additional comments: _____

_____

For more information,
see page 63.

EVALUATION GUIDE INSTITUTIONAL EXECUTOR OR TRUSTEE

Name of Nominee: _____

Review Date: _____

Rating System: 1 (unsatisfactory) to 10 (excellent)

Evaluation Areas	Rating
Experience	_____
Reputation	_____
Educational background of employees	_____
Size of organization	_____
Quality of person with whom you deal	_____
General attitude	_____
Fiscal soundness	_____
Other _____	_____
_____	_____
_____	_____
TOTAL	_____

Strong points: _____
_____

Weak points: _____
_____

Additional comments: _____
_____

For more information, see page 64.

EVALUATION GUIDE: GUARDIAN OF THE PERSON

Name of Potential Guardian: _____

Review Date: _____

Rating System: 1 (unsatisfactory) to 10 (excellent)

Evaluation Areas	Rating
Maturity and experience	_____
Temperament	_____
Stamina	_____
Integrity	_____
Stability	_____
Home environment	_____
Financial resources	_____
Ability to relate to your children	_____
Health	_____
Others _____	_____
_____	_____
_____	_____
TOTAL	_____

Strong points: _____

_____

Weak points: _____

_____

Additional comments: _____

_____

For more information, see page 68.

EVALUATION GUIDE: GUARDIAN OF THE ESTATE

Name of Potential Guardian: _____

Review Date: _____

Rating System: 1 (unsatisfactory) to 10 (excellent)

Evaluation Areas	Rating
Financial knowledge	_____
General business background	_____
Fee structure	_____
Maturity and experience	_____
Integrity	_____
Stability	_____
Ability to relate to your children	_____
Health	_____
Others _____	_____
_____	_____
_____	_____
TOTAL	_____

Strong points: _____

_____

Weak points: _____

_____

Additional comments: _____

_____

For more information, see page 68.

TRUSTEE EVALUATION GUIDE

Name of Potential Trustee: _____

Review Date: _____

Rating System: 1 (unsatisfactory) to 10 (excellent)

Evaluation Areas	Rating
Financial knowledge	_____
Maturity and experience	_____
Stability	_____
Integrity	_____
Business background	_____
Fee structure	_____
Ability to relate to your children	_____
Health	_____
TOTAL	_____

Strong points: _____

_____

Weak points: _____

_____

Additional comments: _____

_____

For more information,
see page 69.

CHILDPROOF PROTECTION SUMMARY

Primary Guardian: _____

Secondary Guardian: _____

Primary Trustee: _____

Secondary Trustee: _____

Date of Current Will: _____

*Review of Will
and Tax Provisions:* _____

_____

_____

Child's Name	Distribution of Funds (% or $ Amounts)					
	Age	Amt.	Age	Amt.	Age	Amt.
_____	___	___	___	___	___	___
_____	___	___	___	___	___	___
_____	___	___	___	___	___	___
_____	___	___	___	___	___	___

Special Provision Reminders

1. Is there provision for emergency medical treatment?
2. Is there flexibility for other emergency funds?
3. Is there an adequate allotment for guardians?
4. Has a health problem developed requiring new provisions?
5. Have tax laws recently changed?

For more information,
see page 70.

LIFE INSURANCE WORKSHEET

Immediate Cash Needs	Amount
Pay off debts	$ _____
Pay medical bills (*Not covered by insurance*)	_____
Emergency funds needed	_____
Federal or state estate taxes	_____
Other _____	_____
TOTAL	$ _____

Monthly Cash Needs	
Continuing monthly expenses	$ _____
Replace loss of income	_____
Income for dependents	_____
Additional housekeeping expenses	_____
Other _____	_____
TOTAL	$ _____

Long-Term Cash Needs	
Savings	$ _____
Retirement	_____
College funds	_____
Lump-sum payments to dependents	_____
Other _____	_____
TOTAL	$ _____

LIFE INSURANCE WORKSHEET (Cont.)

Summary of Cash Needs

Immediate Cash $ _____

Monthly cash
a. *Multiply monthly income by 12 to get annual needs*
b. *Multiply annual by number of years you want to provide*   _____

Long-term cash   _____

TOTAL CASH NEEDS $ _____

Value of Other Assets $ _____
(see Worksheets #s14–19)

Life Insurance Needs $ _____
(Cash needs less assets)

For more information,
see page 71.

DEPENDENT INCOME WORKSHEET

Monthly Income

Dependent	Monthly Amount	Number of Years
	$_____	_____
_____	_____	_____
_____	_____	_____
_____	_____	_____
_____	_____	_____
_____	_____	_____
_____	_____	_____
_____	_____	_____
_____	_____	_____

TOTAL $_____

Lump Sum Payments

Dependent	Amount
_____	_____
_____	_____
_____	_____
_____	_____

DEPENDENT INCOME WORKSHEET (Cont.)

Monthly Income

_____ _____

_____ _____

_____ _____

TOTAL $_____

For more information,
see page 74.

BENEFICIARY WORKSHEET

Name	Relationship	Total Amount of Money I Want Them to Have	Specific Assets I Want Them to Have

For more information, see page 74.

Comprehensive Medical Care

Deductible: Per Individual _____ *Per Family* _____

Calendar Year _____ *Per Condition* _____

Maximum Limit _____

Basic Surgical

Maximum Limit _____

Surgical Schedule: _____

_____ *Reasonable and Customary*

_____ *Relative Value Schedule*

_____ *Specific Limits*

_____ *In or Out of Hospital*

_____ *Doctor's Office*

Basic Hospital

Daily Limit _____

Number of Days _____

Maximum Limit _____

Deductible: Per Individual _____ *Per Family* _____

Calendar Year _____ *Per Condition* _____

*Miscellaneous Hospital
Expense Limit* _____

Hospital Confinement

Deductible _____

Daily Limit _____

Maximum Limit _____

MEDICAL INSURANCE COVERAGE WORKSHEET (Cont.)

Major Medical

Maximum Limit _____

Deductible: Per Individual _____ *Per Family* _____

Calendar Year _____ *Per Condition* _____

Excess Major Medical

Maximum _____

Deductible: Per Individual _____ *Per Family* _____

Calendar Year _____ *Per Condition* _____

Special Clauses—Does your policy include:

	Yes	No
Pre-existing condition	[ ]	[ ]
Dependents		
a. Until age ___	[ ]	[ ]
b. Residing at home	[ ]	[ ]
Nursing care	[ ]	[ ]
Home care (nurses and therapists)	[ ]	[ ]
Nursing homes	[ ]	[ ]
Maternity benefits	[ ]	[ ]
Prevailing rate clause	[ ]	[ ]
Second-opinion surgery	[ ]	[ ]
30-day conversion clause	[ ]	[ ]
Noncancelable clause	[ ]	[ ]
Guaranteed renewable	[ ]	[ ]
Hospital pre-authorization clause	[ ]	[ ]

MEDICAL INSURANCE COVERAGE WORKSHEET (Cont.)

Special Clauses—Does your policy include: Yes   No

Psychological coverage   [ ]   [ ]

Spousal conversion   [ ]   [ ]

Accidental death   [ ]   [ ]

Life insurance   [ ]   [ ]

For more information,
see page 86.

MEDICAL INSURANCE COST/COVERAGE COMPARISON

Type of Coverage	Insurance Co. No. 1		Insurance Co. No. 2	
	Premium	Coverage	Premium	Coverage
Basic Medical Expense	$ _____	_____	$ _____	_____
Maximum Limit		_____		_____
Deductible		_____		_____
Basic Surgical Expense	$ _____	_____	$ _____	_____
Maximum Limit		_____		_____
Deductible		_____		_____
Basic Hospital Expense	$ _____	_____	$ _____	_____
Daily Limit		_____		_____
Number of Days		_____		_____
Maximum Limit		_____		_____
Deductible		_____		_____

MEDICAL INSURANCE COST/COVERAGE COMPARISON (Cont.)

Type of Coverage	Insurance Co. No. 1		Insurance Co. No. 2	
	Premium	Coverage	Premium	Coverage
Hospital Confinement	$ _____	_____	$ _____	_____
Daily Limit	_____	_____	_____	_____
Maximum Limit	_____	_____	_____	_____
Deductible	_____	_____	_____	_____
Major Medical	$ _____	_____	$ _____	_____
Limit	_____	_____	_____	_____
Deductible	_____	_____	_____	_____
Excess Major Medical	$ _____	_____	$ _____	_____
Limit	_____	_____	_____	_____
Deductible	_____	_____	_____	_____
Medicare Supplement	$ _____	_____	$ _____	_____
Amount	_____	_____	_____	_____

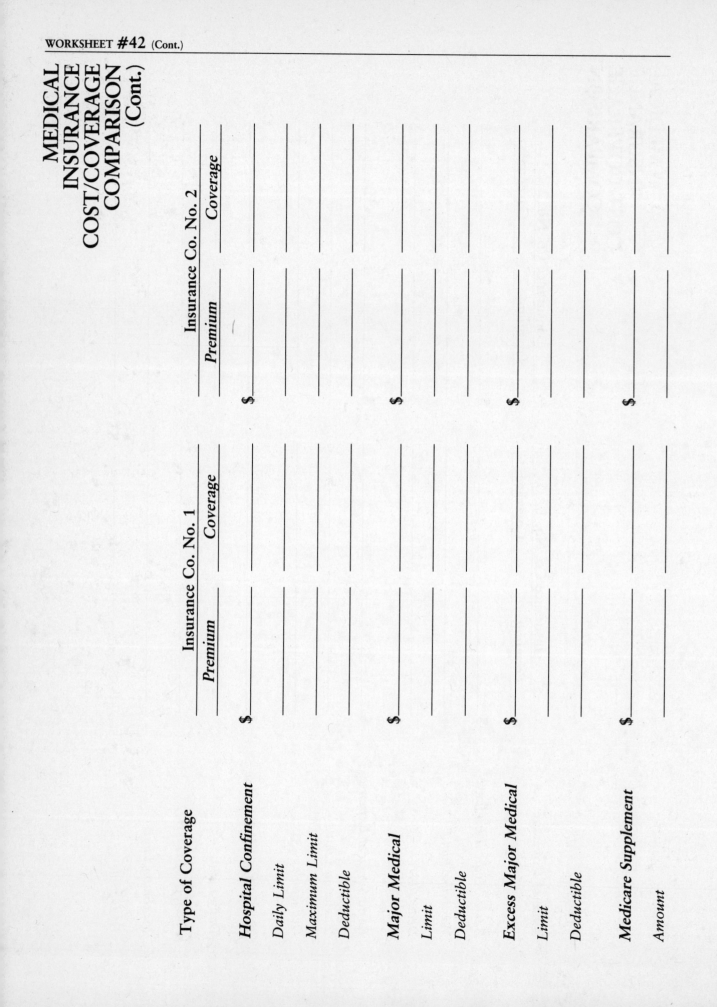

MEDICAL INSURANCE COST/COVERAGE COMPARISON (Cont.)

For more information, see page 86.

Accident Only

$ _____ $ _____

Amount

_____   _____

Specific Diseases

$ _____ $ _____

Amount

$ _____ $ _____

Remarks: _____

_____

_____

EVALUATING HMO AND GROUP INSURANCE

Potential Health Maintenance Organization: _____

Potential Insurance Company: _____

Rating: 1 (unsatisfactory) to 10 (excellent)

Evaluation Areas	HMO	Insurance Company
Basic hospital coverage	_____	_____
Basic surgical coverage	_____	_____
Coverage deductible	_____	_____
Training of physicians in general	_____	_____
Ability of physicians to relate to you	_____	_____
Convenience of location	_____	_____
Quality of area where located	_____	_____
Size of company	_____	_____
Appearance of office	_____	_____
Outside local area benefits	_____	_____
TOTALS	_____	_____

EVALUATING HMO AND GROUP INSURANCE (Cont.)

	HMO	Insurance Company
General comments:	_____	_____
	_____	_____
	_____	_____
	_____	_____
	_____	_____
	_____	_____
Strong points:	_____	_____
	_____	_____
	_____	_____
	_____	_____
	_____	_____
	_____	_____
Weak points:	_____	_____
	_____	_____
	_____	_____
	_____	_____
	_____	_____

For more information, see page 87.

DISABILITY INSURANCE CHECKLIST

	Yes	No

1. *How does policy define disability:*

   a. *Can you perform your particular job?*　　　[　]　　[　]

   b. *Can you work at any occupation?*　　　[　]　　[　]

   c. *Would you lose money if you worked part-time?*　　　[　]　　[　]

   d. *Must you be totally hospitalized for benefits?*　[　]　[　]

   e. *Must you be totally house-bound for benefits?*　[　]　[　]

   f. *Other* _____　[　]　[　]

2. *Is the policy guaranteed renewable?*　　[　]　　[　]

3. *Is there a waiting period before payments begin?*　[　]　[　]

4. *Is there an employment eligibility period?*　[　]　[　]

5. *Is there a "survivor" benefit?*　　[　]　　[　]

6. *Is there a mental illness exclusion?*　　[　]　　[　]

7. *Must you pay premiums while receiving disability payments?*　　　[　]　　[　]

8. *Is there a rehabilitative benefit?*　　[　]　　[　]

9. *Are benefits reduced if you have other sources of income?*　　　[　]　　[　]

   Earned [　]　　*Unearned* [　]　　*Social Security* [　]
   Workers Compensation [　]

10. *What is the elimination period?*
    30 days [　]　*60 days* [　]　*90 days* [　]　*Over 90 days* [　]

11. *Benefits are based on:*

    a. *Length of service* [　] _____

    b. *Salary* 　　　　[　] _____

DISABILITY INSURANCE CHECKLIST (Cont.)

12. *How long do the payments last?*

  a. *For sickness:* _____

  b. *For accident:* _____

  c. *What are the total monthly benefits?* _____

  d. *What is the maximum benefit payable?* _____

For more information, see page 91.

EMERGENCY DISABILITY PLAN

Plan arranged as of

_____

I. **Ready Cash** — **Estimated Amounts**

A. *Primary sources*

1. *Disability insurance* — $_____

2. *Social Security or state disability benefits* — _____

3. *Money market funds* — _____

4. *Savings account* — _____

5. *Cashable securities (stocks and bonds)* — _____

6. *Bank loans (pre-arranged)* — _____

7. *Regular checking account* — _____

8. *Checking account overdraft protection* — _____

9. *Credit card limits* — _____

Cash from primary sources — $_____

B. *Secondary sources*

1. *Borrow on the cash value of life insurance policies* — $_____

2. *Borrow from profit-sharing plan* — _____

3. *Borrow from credit union* — _____

4. *Borrow from personal loan companies* — _____

5. *Secure loan on the car or increase present loan* — _____

6. *Secure cash from Keogh or IRA account* — _____

EMERGENCY DISABILITY PLAN
(Cont.)

Plan arranged as of

_____

I. Ready Cash   **Estimated Amounts**

7. *Take out a second or third mortgage on the home* _____

8. *Notify employer to change your federal withholding* _____

9. *Creditor loans* _____

10. *Pawn jewelry* _____

11. *Sell collections* _____

12. *Borrow from friends or relatives* _____

13. *Secure loan from employer* _____

14. *Sell second car* _____

15. *Other* _____ _____

          Cash from secondary sources $_____

          TOTAL READY CASH $_____

II. Expenses   **Monthly Amount**

    A. *New Expenses*

       1. *Medical costs*

          a. Hospital costs not covered by insurance $_____

          b. Doctors' fees not covered by insurance _____

          c. Private nursing _____

          d. Drugs and miscellaneous _____

II. Expenses   **Monthly Amount**

EMERGENCY DISABILITY PLAN (Cont.)

Plan arranged as of

    2. *Other expenses*

        a. Transportation   _____   _____

        b. House expenses   _____

             1. New household maintenance expenses   _____

             2. Extra baby-sitting because of your absence   _____

        c. Others

             1. _____   _____

             2. _____   _____

             3. _____   _____

             4. _____   _____

B. *Regular Monthly Expenses (from budget)*   _____

    TOTAL MONTHLY EXPENSES   **$**_____

III. **Emergency Action Plans During This Period**

    A. *List all expenses you can reduce during this period:*

        1. _____

        2. _____

        3. _____

        4. _____

        5. _____

EMERGENCY DISABILITY PLAN
(Cont.)

Plan arranged as of

_____

III. Emergency Action Plans During This Period

    B. *List all creditors who would extend payment period:*

        1. _____

        2. _____

        3. _____

        4. _____

        5. _____

    C. *Notify the disability insurance company to begin benefits.*

    D. *Recheck your medical insurance so you know exactly what the deductibles and coverages are.*

    E. *Determine which friends, relatives, and neighbors will assist you with certain functions.*

    F. *Notify the children's schools of problems at home.*

    G. *Contact community support groups, such as United Way, for information regarding assistance with transportation, visiting nurses, etc.*

    H. _____

    I. _____

    J. _____

    K. _____

For more information, see page 93.

LONG-TERM DISABILITY PLAN

As of

_____

1. Sources of Income   Estimated Amounts

    A. *Monthly income from disability insurance* $_____

    B. *Monthly income from 90-day emergency plan* $_____

    C. *Other sources of monthly income*

      _____ _____

      _____ _____

      _____ _____

      TOTAL MONTHLY INCOME $_____

      TOTAL AUSTERITY BUDGET $_____

      CASH NEEDS $_____

2. Pre-arranged Expense Reduction   Amount of Decrease

    1. _____ $_____

    2. _____ _____

    3. _____ _____

    4. _____ _____

    5. _____ _____

    6. _____ _____

    7. _____ _____

    8. _____ _____

    TOTAL MONTHLY AUSTERITY BUDGET $_____

    TOTAL MONTHLY INCOME $_____

    TOTAL MONTHLY CASH NEEDS $_____

LONG-TERM DISABILITY PLAN
(Cont.)

As of

_____

3. Potential Income Sources

Estimated Amounts

	Estimated Amounts
A. *Wife works full or part-time*	$_____
B. *Children work part-time*	_____
C. *Establish a home business*	_____
D. _____	_____
E. _____	_____
F. _____	_____
G. _____	_____

TOTAL $_____

For more information,
see page 94.

TRANSITION PLAN CHECKLIST
At Once

		Completed
1.	*Make funeral arrangements*	[ ]
2.	*Decide on obituary notices*	[ ]
3.	*Notify relatives*	[ ]
4.	*Notify friends*	[ ]
5.	*Open a new checking account in your name*	[ ]

Within the First 30 Days

		Completed
1.	*Get 20 certified copies of the death certificate*	[ ]
2.	*Put all joint checking and savings accounts in your name*	[ ]
3.	*Establish an "estate" bank account*	[ ]
4.	*Notify all insurance companies involved and file claims*	[ ]
5.	*Review the auto insurance for accidental death, medical, or other coverages*	[ ]
6.	*Check the medical policies for any time limitations for filing claims and for additional coverages*	[ ]
7.	*Check for travel accident coverage*	[ ]
8.	*Report death to Social Security*	[ ]
9.	*Apply for Social Security benefits*	[ ]
10.	*Report death to Veteran's Administration and apply for benefits*	[ ]
11.	*Notify spouse's employers or associates to file for benefits*	[ ]
12.	*Check on Workers Compensation benefits*	[ ]
13.	*Check spouse's possible life insurance coverage with clubs, associations, credit cards, or other organizations*	[ ]

TRANSITION PLAN CHECKLIST (Cont.)

Completed

14. *Have securities transferred to your name*   [   ]

15. *Have U.S. Savings Bonds placed in your name*   [   ]

16. *Open a safe-deposit box in your name*   [   ]

17. *Notify IRA and Keogh accounts*   [   ]

18. *Review Chapter 5, Borrowing*   [   ]

19. *Review income tax records*   [   ]

20. Other _____   [   ]

21. Other _____   [   ]

22. Other _____   [   ]

23. Other _____   [   ]

24. Other _____   [   ]

25. Other _____   [   ]

TRANSITION PLAN CHECKLIST (Cont.)

Within the Next 60 Days

Completed

1. *Select an attorney to represent your interest and to file the will*   [   ]

2. *Pick an accountant for financial affairs and for filing estate and inheritance tax returns*   [   ]

3. *Transfer real estate title to your name*   [   ]

4. *Transfer title on cars to your name*   [   ]